E COLLEGE OF
HARD COLLYER
BUSINESS HANDBOOKS

If you are running your own business then you probably do not have time for the general, theoretical and often impenetrable subject areas covered by many business and management books. What works for the major corporation may not work for you. What you do need is to-the-point guidance on how to implement sound business skills in a growing enterprise.

The NatWest Business Handbooks deliver this practical advice in an easy-to-follow format.

Written by authors with many years' experience and who are still actively involved in the day-to-day running of successful businesses, these handbooks provide all the guidance you need to tackle the everyday issues that you and your business face. They will enable you to adopt a step-by-step approach to isolating and resolving problems and help you meet the entrepreneurial and organisational challenges of a growing business.

♻ NatWest

BUSINESS HANDBOOKS

STARTING UP

How to launch and grow the new business

Fourth Edition

GARY JONES

PEARSON EDUCATION LIMITED

Head Office:
Edinburgh Gate
Harlow CM20 2JE
Tel: +44 (0)1279 623623
Fax: +44 (0)1279 431059

London Office:
128 Long Acre, London WC2E 9AN
Tel: +44 (0)171 447 2000
Fax: +44 (0)171 240 5771

First published in Great Britain 1988
Fourth edition 1998

© Financial Times Professional Limited 1998

The right of Gary Jones to be identified as
Author of this Work has been asserted by him in accordance
with the Copyright, Designs, and Patents Act 1988.

ISBN 0 273 63563 8

British Library Cataloguing in Publication Data
A CIP catalogue record for this book can be obtained from the British Library.

10 9 8 7 6 5 4 3

Typeset by Northern Phototypesetting Co. Ltd, Bolton
Printed and bound in Great Britain by Bell & Bain Ltd, Glasgow

The Publishers' policy is to use paper manufactured from sustainable forests.

About the Author

Gary Jones is Lecturer in Information Technology and Computing and a freelance web designer. He has extensive experience in web design and Internet programming. He has lectured on numerous courses, and advised and worked on a number of projects for national examining bodies. He also has considerable business experience in retail management, ran his own small business, and is the author of *Running a Shop and Marketing Decisions*.

To Doris, Andrea, Nick and my Dad.

Contents

Preface

Thinking about starting up in business?
Planning to expand your business?
Wondering how the Internet may affect your business?
Confused by other books?

This book has been designed for you. It will help you understand and plan what has to be done in plain and clear language.

This edition includes a new chapter on the Internet and its importance to small- to medium-sized enterprises (SMEs). It explains in clear terms what the Internet is and how it works, and moves quickly on to examine both the opportunities and pitfalls for SMEs. There is guidance on how to exploit the Internet to the benefit of your business and checklists to help you plan and publish your business web site.

Also new for this edition is a support web site for *Starting Up*. It features:

- a directory of links to information and resources for SMEs and business start ups;
- spreadsheets to download to help you forecast cash needs and make profit projections;
- frequently asked questions and answers;
- further information and guidance on business web sites.

The *Starting Up Web Site* can be accessed from the main menu at

http://www.ftmanagement.com.

Success and failure in business are not the chance results of the toss of a coin. Being in the right place at the right time is partly luck, but more to do with good planning. Many who become one of the failure statistics simply did not plan. If you use this book intelligently, you should not be one of them, for this book is about small business planning. The book will help you to:

- generate business ideas;
- weigh up the pros and cons of buying an existing business, franchise or starting from scratch;

- select an idea that stands a good chance of success;
- avoid the common mistakes that contribute to early business failure;
- lay out the framework for your business plan;
- identify the market for your business idea;
- refine the idea to match with what customers want;
- win customers and build sales;
- select the right type of premises;
- take steps to ensure the business makes sufficient profit;
- calculate the cash required to keep your business alive and well;
- demystify the working of the Internet;
- identify business uses of the Internet;
- plan a business web site;
- choose a web site designer.

This is very much an 'how to' book supported with step-by-step guidance and fully explained examples. All chapters include comprehensive checklists to help you check your progress and, as far as possible, make sure you don't leave a vital element out of your preparations for starting up. The final chapter contains an overall pre-start-up checklist.

The book is based in part on my own personal experience of managing a number of small businesses, starting my own business, lecturing on courses for SMEs and extensive experience in designing web sites and using Internet technologies. My quest continues to be to give you a practical, usable book that will become a friend in the hard, interesting and, finally, personally and financially rewarding task in front of you.

Gary Jones
July 1998
E-mail: Gary.Jones@ftmanagement.com
Web site: *Starting Up* http://www.ftmanagement.com

Business ideas

1
2
3
4
5
6
7
8
9
10

WHY START YOUR OWN BUSINESS?

Setting up in business for the first time or expanding an existing business can be an exciting experience. It can be the road to riches and personal fulfilment. It can also be the road to financial ruin and personal misery. Successful businesses are, in the main. the result of careful research and planning; enthusiasm, self-confidence and commitment, although essential, are not enough on their own.

Careful consideration should be given to the options for earning a livelihood. For most people the decision is between employment, unemployment and self-employment. What are the advantages and disadvantages of each? What's good about your present situation? What will you be giving up if you start your own business? What will you be gaining?

> *Successful businesses are, in the main, the result of careful research and planning.*

To help you weigh up the alternatives, consider the experiences of two people who recently started their own small businesses:

'... it's been good to get away from the petty bickering at work ... nobody breathing down your neck every minute of the day ... above all else, I enjoy taking the responsibility, making the decisions – when they have come off it has brought a great sense of achievement and sometimes relief – when they haven't, solving the problems has been a challenge ... being in business is about solving problems ... it was hard at first, the hours are still long but the business is doing well and I should be reaping the financial dividends by the end of next year...'

'... to begin with I expected to work hard; however, the pace hasn't slackened – in fact it's got worse – I find it difficult to keep track of all aspects of the business – you know, the accounts, letters, finding new customers, and there always seem to be problems with suppliers. I've had a lot of trouble finding enough cash to keep the business afloat – sales have not grown fast enough, but the bills keep coming in ... the bank would not lend me any more money without a legal charge on my house – if the business fails I will lose everything. Sometimes the worry

is too much. There have been many times when I've not been able to sleep at night. I've no family and social life any more – the business takes up too much time – one of the bad moments was six months ago, I was very ill with flu for two weeks. There was no way I could have stayed in bed – the business would have folded.'

Exercise

Take a sheet of paper and list about five advantages and five disadvantages of your present situation. Then do the same for a business venture you have in mind.

How do the options balance out – is starting your own business the right alternative for you?

What qualities do you think you need to succeed?

HOW CAN I FIND A 'GOOD' BUSINESS IDEA?

It is likely that you have already decided to some extent what business you would like to start. However, you may be at the stage where you would welcome the opportunity to run your own business but are not sure in which direction to go. The following sections will help you to generate more business ideas and consider them in relation to your own motivation, interests, needs, skills and resources.

There is a multitude of business opportunities to choose from, ranging from home-based ideas, such as furniture repairs, dress- and curtain-making or growing decorative plants, through offering standard services, such as domestic cleaning, car repairs, painting and decorating, to running a shop, restaurant, rest home or hotel. Maybe you are considering something larger, presenting a more difficult challenge, such as manufacturing.

There are no 'magic formulas' for generating business ideas. However, the following activities will help you draw up a range, all of them proving more fruitful if you attempt them with a friend.

■ Building on your skills, hobbies or interests

Take five minutes to list as many of your interests and skills as you can think of. For each, try to think of a business idea to match it. Here is an example.

Interests/skills	Business idea
Hiking	Guided country walks
Cooking	Home catering; restaurant
Meeting people	Taxi proprietor; retailing

■ Having problems?

If you are struggling to find business ideas, use publications such as *Business Ideas*, *Exchange and Mart*, the classified section of your local paper, the *Yellow Pages* or British Telecom's *Business to Business* directory to make a list that appeals to you. Use it to identify any ideas that match up with your own skills or interests.

■ Copying or improving somebody else's successful idea

It is a common fallacy that for a business to be a success it must be based on an innovative and original idea. In fact the opposite can be true: the less the idea has already been tried and tested by other entrepreneurs, the greater the element of risk.

Make a list of the businesses in your area that appear to be successful. Do any appeal to you?

Can you improve on any already established businesses? For the existing businesses that appeal to you, try to make a list of the things that they do badly. How could you alter that business to improve on it?

■ Spotting a gap in the market

Many of today's successful businesspeople have got where they have by identifying and exploiting a 'gap' in a fast-growing market. It is a matter of identifying needs of sections of the market that are presently not met by existing businesses. Virgin Airlines established itself by meeting the need of a large section of the travelling public for cheap air travel. Club 18–30 provides holidays for the under-30s. A recent and more novel idea was the launch of a free newspaper for the 'rich', which provided a successful business for its originators by selling advertising space to manufacturers of 'quality' high-priced products.

Spotting a gap in the market is not necessarily easy. Here are some suggestions for how you could attempt this.

Exercise Try to identify current national and local trends. The HMSO publication *Social Trends* (found in the reference section of most public libraries) can be an invaluable source of such information, as can local and national newspapers, and TV news and current affairs programmes, such as *The Money Programme* (BBC 2).

Having identified what you think are some interesting trends, try to translate them into possible business ideas by identifying a possible market need each suggests and a business idea that feasibly might meet that need. For example:

Trend	Need	Possible business idea
Increase in crime against the person	Greater personal security	Home security services or products Personal security service or products Self-defence classes
Increase in single-parent families	Occasional freedom from pressure of looking after their children	Baby-sitting service Safe transport and supervision of children to and from school Setting up of town centre nursery to enable the parent to shop or go to work

etc ....

Listen to what people say. Many times you will hear people say such things as 'if only ...

they stocked ...'
there was a cheap ...'
there was a decent bus service between ...'

you could rely on "them", I would pay to have "it" done ...'
they opened late I would use them more often ...'

If enough people say the same thing there *might* be a gap in the market.

....

Of course, you would have to research whether or not any market need or gap you discover is already sufficiently met in your area. As with all initial business ideas, proceed with caution. Do not assume too much from limited information.

IS IT A GOOD IDEA?

I hope the preceding activities have enabled you to compile a list of possible business ideas for you to explore. At some stage you must decide on which idea to investigate further. The factors that affect your final choice from a short list of potential business ideas can be split broadly into personal and business considerations.

■ Personal considerations

■ *Your skills – can you do it?*

When starting a business, many people wish to capitalise on existing skills. If this is an important consideration for you, carefully consider each business idea on your list in relation to your skills.

Perhaps you do not consider this an important factor. New skills and knowledge can be obtained by a number of means. Your local further education college or adult education centre will probably be able to offer you a course in your area of need. Alternatively, or to support your doing a course, you may be able to seek temporary employment in a business of your choice, gaining the skills and knowledge first-hand.

> *'Will I like the "work" the business involves?'*

■ *Your interests*

An important question to ask yourself is, 'Will I like the "work" the business involves?' There is little point in establishing a business that involves a considerable amount of work that you don't enjoy or even detest. For each of your possible business ideas, try to identify what daily work activities it will involve. If you don't know, find out – again, by taking temporary or part-time work in that area or, if that is not possible, by talking to and observing people in that type of business.

■ *Your personal commitments*

It is important to have the support of your family and friends. Are they prepared to put up with you spending evenings and weekends helping your business grow? If not, look for a less demanding form of business.

■ Business considerations

■ *Is there a market for your product or service?*

This is of paramount importance. Without a sufficient market for your product or service, your business is doomed before it starts. Chapter 3 deals in detail with market research, but, initially, you must be able to answer roughly some of the following basic questions in relation to your selected business ideas.

- Who will buy your product or service?
- Why will they buy from you instead of the competition?
- How big is the market?
- What will your share be?
- Is the market over-supplied?
- Is the market growing or contracting?

■ *How much capital will the business require – can you afford it?*

This is obviously an important consideration. Chapter 7 will help you calculate the amount you will require to start the business. Chapter 8 will tell you where you can obtain finance and how to go about raising it. As a rough guide, most financial institutions will require you to put up nearly half the total requirement of the business venture. As regards what it will cost (see Chapter 6), service businesses tend to be cheaper to set up than those involving specialised premises and expensive equipment.

At this stage, it is important to have a clear idea of the amount of personal capital you can raise.

Make a list of your assets.

- House value — How much personal capital do you have tied up in your house? Make a conservative estimate of the market value of your house and subtract the balance of your mortgage that is outstanding. *Note:* you can remortgage your house – usually up to 80 per cent of its value.

- Life assurance policies — You can obtain a quote on their current surrender value. *Whether or not this is a sensible financial decision needs careful consideration.*

- Material possessions — For instance, you may have a new car that you can sell and replace with a cheaper second-hand one.

- Shares
- Premium bonds
- Savings accounts

Coming to a final decision involves weighing up all the above considerations. It will help you to have some objective method of bringing them all together. Choosing a business is similar to choosing a house. Try the followingexercise.

Make a list of what you require from a business venture. This might include items such as:

- regular hours
- flexible hours
- no unsocial hours
- high degree of profits
- low capital requirements
- no need to employ people
- does not involve personal selling

- meeting people
- little paperwork
- will exploit existing skills
- involves working outdoors
- will provide potential for expansion
- involves travelling
- involves working from home
- will not require expensive premises
- involves little risk.

Consider your list and decide which are the most important and least important requirements. To make it clearer, give each requirement a weighting to signify how important it is, for instance from 1 to 10 (the more important the requirement is, the higher the score you give it).

To illustrate this method, take the example of Ann, who had two young children at school and little capital. She wanted to run a small business that would give her sufficient income, but, more importantly, she wanted to gain a sense of achievement and fulfilment from what she did. She also wanted to meet people and 'broaden her horizons'. She had some skills in sewing and claimed to have an eye for fashion, having made some of her children's clothes which had drawn favourable comment from her friends.

Ann's list of requirements for a business venture looked like this:

Requirement	Importance
Low capital required (below £2500)	10
Flexible hours	9
Able to work from home	4
Interest/satisfaction	7
Able to meet people	9

Low capital was very important because of the small amount she could raise. As Ann had to take her children to, and pick them up from, school, having decided that the cost of a child minder would be too great, flexible hours or hours that coincided with school hours was also an important consideration.

Ann had drawn up a short list of three business ideas:

- producing soft toys for sale on a rented stall at the local market;
- buying and selling children's wear via a party plan;
- alterations on contract with local fashion shops.

Exercise

The next step is to score each of your business ideas against the weighted requirements. Award points to each business idea from 0 to 10 – high points if it meets the requirement well, low if it does not. Give each business idea a score, marking its success in meeting each requirement by multiplying the points awarded by the importance factor. The overall score is obtained by adding together the scores for each business idea.

Ann's ideas fared as follows:

Requirement	Importance	Soft toys		Children's party plan		Alterations	
		Points	Score	Points	Score	Points	Score
Low capital required (below £2500)	10	3	30	10	100	5	50
Flexible hours	9	2	18	8	72	10	90
Able to work from home	4	4	16	8	32	8	32
Interest/ satisfaction	7	5	35	8	56	4	28
Able to meet people	9	7	63	9	81	3	27
			162		341		227
Total possible score			390		390		390
Percentage of total possible score			41.5%		87%		58%

In the example, the party plan idea appears to be best suited to Ann – scoring the highest and meeting 87 per cent of her requirements.

As a guide, your highest-scoring business must meet well in excess of 50 per cent of your requirements. If it does not, it is suggested that you examine other options or reassess your evaluations of each business.

A note of warning. Although this method is a useful means of ordering your thoughts to help you make a decision, your results will only be as accurate as your evaluations. The method will help ensure that your business is well matched to your personal requirements, but it does not tell you whether or not the business will be a success.

 Checklist

1 Have you the health and stamina for your selected venture?

2 Can you cope with the stresses and strains?

3 Are you prepared to take a calculated risk?

4 How will you cope if the going gets tough both in the planning and running of the business?

5 We all have strengths and weaknesses – what are yours?

6 How are you going to exploit your strong points?

7 What are you going to do about your weak points?

8 Have you the necessary skills?

9 Are you a self-starter?

10 Do you have self-discipline?

11 Can you work long hours over a sustained period?

12 Have you discussed your project with your family and friends?

13 Do you have their support?

14 Have you thought long and hard and identified your reasons for going into business?

15 Have you discussed your responses to this checklist with somebody who knows you well?

SHOULD I BUY AN EXISTING BUSINESS?

Having decided to go into business and selected a potential business idea, the question arises. 'Should I start from scratch or buy an existing business?' If you are one of the few who have a completely new product or service, the decision, by definition, is made for you. For others, the choice is open.

> *'Should I start from scratch or buy an existing business?'*

A major appeal of buying an existing business is speed – the business is a going concern, so, hopefully, revenue will come in from day 1. There is little inconvenience – no looking for suitable premises, choosing equipment or finding new customers and suppliers.

A second and important advantage is that if you have selected your business well, you will have a sound base from which to expand, innovate and perhaps change direction. Starting from scratch, it often takes three to six months to reach a viable sales level. An existing business will have a track record. You can look at past sales records and have an accountant check out its financial viability. When starting from scratch, the risk is greater. Market research can provide good estimates of potential revenue, but cannot guarantee it!

There are disadvantages, however. Starting from scratch can be cheaper, as you are not paying for goodwill. Also, you can often obtain exactly what you require in terms of premises, location, equipment and so on more easily. Buying a business is sometimes like buying a second-hand car or house – there are

Buyers new to business often make the mistake of relying too heavily on the past accounts of the business

unseen flaws. After you take over, you may find that the premises are not really as suitable as you thought – they might be in the wrong place, have the wrong equipment and there may not be sufficient room for expansion. For example, planning permission cannot be gained for an extension.

Buyers new to business often make the mistake of relying too heavily on the past accounts of the business for assurance that it is a viable concern. 'Let the buyer beware' is a saying worth remembering. The problem with records is two-fold.

First, the records refer to what has happened in the past – there is no guarantee that the business will continue to be a success in the future. For instance, the previous owner's business may have been based on personal reputation, so when he goes, so does the business. I know of a young couple who recently purchased a small hotel, the accounts of which showed good past trade. The previous owner purchased another hotel in the same vicinity and took his regular clientele with him. The young couple are now in the position of having to build up their clientele from scratch and, as a consequence, have serious cash flow problems.

Second, accounts can conceal as much as they reveal, and depend for their accuracy on the honesty of the owner of the business. It should also be noted that the accounts do not give the full story. For instance, they do not tell you if double yellow lines are going to be placed outside your newly acquired newsagent's shop or about the large store that is going to open up close by and take away all your trade.

Whether you decide to buy or start from scratch, the detailed research and planning this book sets out is equally applicable to both forms of business start-up.

 Checklist

1 How long would it take to start this business from scratch?

2 What is the cost of starting from scratch?

3 What degree of risk is there in starting from scratch?

4 Why buy an existing business?

5 Look at a range of businesses, go to your local commercial estate agent.

6 How many properties would you look at before making a decision to buy a house?

7 Have you 'viewed' at least this many businesses?

8 Will the vendor provide you with copies of at least three years' accounts?

9 If not, lose interest immediately!

10 What degree of certainty is there that you will retain the business' customers once the present owners depart?

11 Have you deciphered the real reasons for the sale? Don't take the vendor's reasons at face value!

12 What present and future threats and opportunities are there to the business (see Chapter 2).

13 What *exactly* is included in the sale?

14 What is the sales trend (over at least the past three years)?

15 When you subtract inflation from these figures, what does the real trend look like?

16 In relation to present and future customers (see Chapter 3), what is a conservative estimate of its future potential?

17 Compare these sales figures to trends in this sector of business. For example, an increase of 10 per cent in sales when the market has increased by 30 per cent in the same period means the business is contracting not expanding.

18 What is the net profit now, and is it enough for both:
   – personal requirements?
   – reinvestment in the business to enable it to grow?

19 What is the real trend in profits? Look out for unusually high closing stocks – these can artificially push up the profit figure (see Chapter 6).

20 Calculate the net profit as a percentage of the total investment in the business (see Chapters 6 and 7).

21 How many years will the business take to pay for itself? (*Note:* as a rough guide, the business should pay for itself in less than five years.)

22 Have you examined all the overheads?

23 Are they realistic?

24 If stock is included:
   – will the stock sell?
   – how has it been valued?
   – is it a realistic valuation?

25 What is the value of the business' net assets (see Chapter 7)?

26 How does this compare to the asking price?

27 How many years at current profit levels will it take you to cover the asking price?

28 What value, if any, has been placed on 'goodwill'?

29 What was your answer to question 10?

30 What is the ceiling price you are not prepared to exceed?

31 Are there any hidden costs to the purchase (e.g. redecoration costs, replacement of unsuitable equipment)?

32 What points are there for negotiation with the vendor?

33 Can the asking price be brought down?

34 Refer to and apply the 'premises checklist' at the end of Chapter 5.

WHAT IS A FRANCHISE – IS IT A GOOD WAY TO START?

An increasingly popular alternative to starting from scratch or buying an existing business is to buy a franchise. A franchise is a business relationship between a franchisor (owner of a name or method of business) and a franchisee (a local operator of that business). The franchisee agrees to pay the franchisor a certain sum of money for use of the business name or method of doing business or both, usually in the form of an initial fee and some agreed percentage of sales or similar.

The main advantage of starting a business by becoming a franchisee is that you are usually buying a tried and tested method for doing a particular business. Consequently, there should be a greater chance of success than with buying an existing business or starting from scratch.

The franchisor will dictate to varying degrees how the business should be run. Often this will include instructing and advising the franchisee on the product or service range, pricing policy, size and design of premises and sometimes even the style of uniform the employees should wear. A good franchisor will also provide a back-up service, giving advice where applicable on such aspects as management, training, merchandising, accounts and so on. Larger franchisors will usually offer advertising and sales promotion support.

The size of franchise businesses varies considerably. The initial cost of buying a franchise ranges from a few thousand upwards to half a million pounds. Franchising has now become so popular (there are now in excess of 18,000 franchises in the UK) that most of the major clearing banks have set up specialist sections to deal with finance applications from potential franchisees.

The main disadvantage of becoming a franchisee is that the business is never truly yours. As the franchisor lays down certain requirements, which can be quite comprehensive, you can never run the business exactly as you want. If the franchisor is not flexible enough to take into account the changing nature of your local business environment, this lack of control can have adverse effects on your business. Finally, you will never be able to keep all of your profits, as most franchise agreements involve some form of continuing payment to the franchisor related to sales or profits.

Taking up a franchise can be an attractive starting point for those entering into business for the first time. However, beware – not all franchise operations are the same. As a guide to investigating a franchise, use the checklist below. If the franchise is worth purchasing, you must receive satisfactory answers to each question on the checklist.

 Checklist

The franchise operation and operator

1 How long has the franchisor been operating in the UK?

2 How many outlets are in operation? How many have closed and why?

3 Are the present outlets successful? Does the franchise have a good name with its customers and operators?

4 Will this type of business be successful in your area? Is there a viable market in your area?

5 What is the competition in your area?

6 Is the franchise operating in an expanding or contracting market? Is it keeping pace with changes in the market?

7 Is the franchisor a member of the British Franchise Association?

8 What is the financial position of the franchisor? Obtain a copy of the audited accounts.

9 Will the franchisor allow you to take up references on them?

The franchise agreement

1 What is the initial payment – what does it entitle you to?

2 What will your liability be for the payment of royalties?

3 On what conditions can/will the franchise be terminated?

4 What will the franchisor contract to provide?

5 Are there minimum sales figures to be met?

■ Finance

The clearing banks have recognised the importance of franchising as a means of helping individuals to become independent businesspeople. It is not very often that individuals will have cash available to finance their investment in a chosen franchise and many would argue that it would be better for franchisees to take on some level of debt, which will have to be serviced as a result of their efforts.

In ordinary business start-ups, it is not uncommon for assistance from the lender to be limited to 50 per cent of start-up costs. This reflects the uncertainties associated with new ventures – in particular with regard to potential demand, revenue forecasts and so on.

In the case of a proven business format franchise, however, many of these uncertainties are removed because the system has been shown to work. That being so, the level of assistance from a bank in relation to the proprietor's involvement can often justifiably be increased, perhaps to a maximum ratio of 2:1, also with possible reduction in security needed. Borrowing in excess of these guidelines produces a heavy burden on profits in the form of interest payments. Experience shows that the business is then greatly disadvantaged from the outset.

Generally speaking, therefore, your research should be confined to franchises where the total level of investment required is not more than three times the cash you put in – that is, the amount of borrowed money is not more than twice the cash input. In this respect, full start-up costs should be gauged as accurately as possible. Often franchisors' prospectuses only list basic costs.

Financial projections provided by franchisors should be checked independently, by an accountant. The basis on which they have been produced should be established. Any cash flow projections (see Chapter 7) should take into account the cost of any bank borrowing and loan repayments in addition to the franchisee's personal expenditure requirements.

The loan facilities agreed are most commonly taken in the form of specifically structured loans with additional overdraft facilities for working capital purposes. The loans may include such features as fixed monthly repayments and fixed interest rates to ease budgeting, plus a capital repayment holiday in the early stages of the business' development.

Special finance schemes may have been agreed by the banks with specific franchisors and these will usually apply where the franchisor company has a good track record in franchising, its financial position is sound and its management capability is strong.

Further information on franchises can be obtained from The British Franchise Association, Franchise Chambers, Thames View, Newton Road, Henley-on-Thames, Oxon RG9 1HG (tel. 01491 578049). The Association produces a pack advising on all aspects of purchasing and operating a franchise, including a list of all franchisors registered with the Association. The fee for the pack is currently only a few pounds and is obtainable at the above address by return post.

SUMMARY

If you didn't have a business idea before you started this chapter, I hope the activities have helped you to generate some new and interesting ones for further consideration. If you already had a good idea about what you would like to do, some of the other activities should have made you pause for thought and make sure that the idea matches your personal requirements and resources.

The rest of the book is about researching and planning the business venture in more detail. The next chapter will introduce you to the importance of planning, the mistakes that many new businesses make – and help you to get organised for the interesting and demanding task ahead.

The plan of action

Introduction • Why do so many new businesses fail?

Marketing • Finance and investment

Organisation and control

Making a start at the planning process – problems and constraints

What are the threats and opportunities to the idea?

The completed plan • Summary

INTRODUCTION

This chapter discusses some of the common mistakes made by new businesses and, in so doing, emphasises the importance of completing a detailed business plan before opening for business. You will also be given a framework around which you can build your business plan; the detail can be added to the framework

> *Good business planning enables growth and increased profitability in times of boom and ensures survival in the lean years.*

as you work through the later chapters in the book. Much emphasis is placed on looking to the future, with the aim of spotting both threats and opportunities. The aim is to make sure you will always survive in times of recession and grow in times of boom.

WHY DO SO MANY NEW BUSINESSES FAIL?

Sales and profits have been squeezed and many more businesses have entered the failure statistics. However, business failures cannot be blamed solely on the ups and downs of the economy. Even in 'good years' thousands of businesses will fail. The real problem is that far too many businesses don't bother to take the trouble to undertake serious and effective business planning. Good business planning enables growth and increased profitability in times of boom and ensures survival in the lean years.

The pity is that most people will plan their holidays but not their business. Would you set out on your holidays not knowing where you were going, what route or transport to take, how much it will cost to get there, whether or not there will be accommodation at the end of your journey and how long you will spend at each place? Perhaps such a holiday may appeal to the wildly adventurous – but would you go into business in this way? It sounds absurd, but many businesspeople proceed exactly like this, muddling through from one day to the next. The 'adventure' usually ends in bankruptcy and in some of the worst cases prison for fraudulent trading.

We can begin to understand what a good business plan should be about by examining the mistakes people make. These can be categorised under the general headings of:

- marketing
- finance and investment
- organisation and control

MARKETING

■ Trying to sell what nobody wants to buy

This is just one of the symptoms resulting from lack of knowledge about the business' market. Market research is essential if you are to avoid this basic sin. As you will discover in the next chapter, marketing is about developing a product and service that customers want to buy, rather than a product you want to sell. Too many start with the product first and then attempt to find customers. This is definitely putting the cart before the horse!

■ Insufficient sales

This is part of the same problem. Many enter into business with no valid and reliable projection of the first year's sales. Without such a projection it is impossible to know:

- what scale of operation you should commit yourself to;
- how much cash you will need, and when, to keep your business alive;
- what profits you will make.

It's like taking a job without asking what you will be paid, then hoping for the best!

■ Overemphasis on price

Many small businesses believe that price is all important and end up underpricing their product or service. This blinkers the business to other, often more important, customer-buying motives. For instance, a property repair business attempting to sell on price when its customers consider quality, reliability and speed of service as being more important will not capture much business.

■ Right product, right price, wrong place

Finding the best route to your customers is vitally important. Many businesses have a product at a price that customers want. The problem? They are selling it through the wrong intermediaries or by the wrong method or in the wrong place.

Your customers will not beat a path to your door simply because you have the right product at the right price. Your customer's decision to buy is influenced just as much by such factors as convenience, accessibility and image of the place from which the product/service is sold.

Do not be tempted, as many other businesspeople have been, to take premises because the rent, rates or purchase price is low or simply because you like the area.

FINANCE AND INVESTMENT

■ Mistaking cash for profit

One of the commonest errors is to mistake cash for profit. Cash and profit are two distinct items. Cash can come from a variety of sources – loans, overdrafts, retained profits and so on. Profits come from the difference between a business' revenue and its costs. Profit can be tied up in stocks and equipment and not necessarily in the form of a growing bank balance. For instance, a

One of the commonest errors is to mistake cash for profit.

business can be making a profit but be overdrawn at the bank because all of its cash is tied up in stock and debtors (people who owe it money). This position is fine if it is controlled, planned for and temporary – it is when this becomes uncontrolled, not planned for and permanent that disaster strikes. Cash is the life-blood of a business and without it raw materials, pay, stock and so on, cannot be funded.

■ Underestimating the investment required

Far too many businesses fail to recognise the length of time it takes to get off the ground. This can vary from three to six months, and even longer with manufacturing businesses. In such cases, the scale of investment required in working capital (cash reserves, stocks, sales made on credit) to keep the business afloat is often overlooked.

■ Full costs of starting up and operating not identified

Many people start up in business without fully realising the size and nature of the hidden costs involved. Often, extravagant purchases are made or certain items purchased outright that would have been better leased. All potential costs should be fully researched and alternative methods of financing considered.

ORGANISATION AND CONTROL

■ No systems or policy for selecting, training and managing staff

Few who start in business for the first time have had experience of selecting, employing and managing staff. Therefore, it is hardly surprising to find that many small businesses and SMEs make costly mistakes in this area. One dishonest or poorly trained employee can cost you all of your profits.

■ Failure to keep records

Ask any businessperson such questions as how this month's sales figures compare with last month's or how much profit was made this month, and the likelihood is that the majority would not be able to give you an accurate answer. They either have not kept up to date with their records or don't have a proper and useful administration system. A business founded and operated on this basis has little chance of success. Without basic accounting information, your business could be nearing failure without you recognising it. You may miss the opportunity to take corrective action.

MAKING A START AT THE PLANNING PROCESS – PROBLEMS AND CONSTRAINTS

■ The problem

Well, what have we learnt from other people's mistakes? First, that business survival and growth – the universal broad aims of all business – are dependent on two key factors:

- Cash resources
- Long-term profitability.

Second, that these two pillars of business can only stem from healthy sales activity. Marketing is therefore in the centre stage. However, just as sales generate profit and cash, they will also soak it up. As they say, 'you don't get something for nothing'.

The problem is maintaining a balance between investment and costs on the one hand and cash and profit generation on the other. Marketing objectives will drive you to invest and expand, while financial objectives will pressurise you to prune and cut back. A good business plan should find the middle road that will

> *The problem is maintaining a balance between investment and costs on the one hand and cash and profit generation on the other.*

lead to planned and steady growth. Overemphasising the importance of either financial or marketing objectives can usher in disaster.

Overzealous pursuit of sales targets can lead you to an 'overtrading' position. This is where investment in increasing sales (that is, product development, additional customer services, more advertising, promotional events and so on) takes out more cash than is being generated, to such an extent that the business becomes insolvent.

Equally, low investment targets can lead to strangulation of the new business at birth. Particularly in times of recession, many businesses seem to develop the commercial equivalent of anorexia. As costs and investment are cut as far as possible, sales falter; further cuts are made, so sales contract further; less cash and profit are generated, which leads to a further round of cut backs, which in turn leads to less cash and profit. So the vicious circle continues until bankruptcy finally buries the business.

■ Know where you are, then you can decide where you want to be

Setting clear and achievable objectives is the key to successful business planning. However, this is easier said than done. To begin with, you will

> *Setting clear and achievable objectives is the key to successful business planning.*

have more questions and problems than answers and solutions. The best way to tackle setting objectives is to map out in some detail your present situation. The logic is that you must identify first where you are before you can decide where you want to be.

The translation of your business idea to a fully fledged business plan will take place within a set of constraints. There will be constraints you have imposed yourself – say, to minimise risk – and constraints that have been imposed on you – for example, by the finance you can raise, the nature of the business you intend to start, local competition, customer preferences and so on. All such factors will limit what you can feasibly do and, therefore, will provide overall limits to your objectives and, as such, guidelines for more detailed planning. Use the following guidelines to define in some detail the constraints you face. Some you may well be able to answer now, while others will have to wait until you have gathered more detailed information. None the less, you will have made a start.

 Checklist

Financial constraints

1 How much personal capital have you at your disposal?

2 How much can you raise in the form of loans?

3 Are you prepared to seek out partners or venture capital?

Constraints relating to personal and risk factors

1 How much do you need to take out of the business for your own personal needs?

2 How many hours are you prepared to work in any week?

3 Are you prepared to work unsocial hours?

4 Do you or your family object to living on the premises?

25

5 How much can you afford or are prepared to lose if the business fails?

6 Will you sacrifice a degree of security to obtain rapid growth?

7 Will you minimise risk by buying an existing business, franchise or start from scratch?

8 What degree of certainty will you require before you decide to start up?

9 Will you want to employ and manage staff or just keep the business as a one-person or family operation?

10 Do you have your family's support?

Marketing constraints

1 Is there a good market for the product or service?

2 What is the minimum (as indicated by competitors) you will have to offer your customers in terms of product/service quality, range, availability, price and additional services to trade successfully?

3 Is demand for the product or service steady or is it subject to ups and downs?

4 Is the market growing or contracting?

5 Are the customers in the market easy or difficult to reach and sell to?

6 Will you have to purchase an existing business or franchise to enter the business selected?

7 How much competition is there?

8 What does the competition offer the customer?

9 Will price levels in the market allow you to trade profitably?

WHAT ARE THE THREATS AND OPPORTUNITIES TO THE IDEA?

In identifying the constraints on your plan, you will have largely determined what you will or can do and what you won't or can't do. The next step is to identify the strengths and weaknesses of your venture in relation to the threats and opportunities posed by the environment in which it will operate. From such an analysis, you will be well placed to set detailed objectives with the aim of minimising risk and maximising opportunity.

The wider business environment is made up of the larger influences of the economy, social trends, population characteristics, laws (present and pending) and developments in technology. These factors, over which you will have little or no control, will directly or indirectly impinge on your day-to-day environment of competing with other businesses, increasing sales, dealing with suppliers and exploiting your business to the full.

The following guidelines will help you identify the threats and opportunities you face.

■ Economic factors

■ *Interest rates*

- By intelligent reading of the quality press, viewing of the more in-depth news programmes, such as *The Money Programme*, *Newsnight* and *Channel 4 News*, what is likely to happen to interest rates in the next 12 months?
- How sensitive are your markets to fluctuations in the rate of interest?
- What percentage of your customers will buy using credit cards, credit sale agreements, bank loans and other forms of finance. Refer to *Social Trends* (HMSO), available at your local library, to find out.
- What effect will 1, 2, 3, 4 and 5 per cent changes in interest rates have on your financial targets?

■ *Inflation*

Prices of all products and services do not go up at the same rate. The various rates of inflation for the different types of products/services you sell and the goods and services your business consumes should be examined for their impact on costs, profits and sales. For example, a high rate of inflation on a product or service where price is an important factor can dramatically curtail sales. Further, if the prices of major items of cost are rising at a greater rate than the price of the items you sell, then profits will be eroded.

- Can increased costs caused by increases in the rate of inflation be passed on to your customers without a marked effect on sales?
- Is your market(s) price-sensitive? (more about this subject in Chapters 3 and 4).

■ In the type of business you are planning to enter, in the past have marked increases in the rate of inflation led to:
- a uniform increase in the market price?
- a price war with the competition?
- increased competition on some other basis, such as offering 0 per cent finance, additional services, improved product quality and so on?

■ *Economic stability*

You should examine the local economies that affect your markets. How prosperous are they? Are they stable, growing or in decline? Such general influences will have some overall impact on the market(s) you serve. Trends in unemployment rates are certainly indicators. Also, if your customers depend on a few large employers for their livelihood, find out how well they are doing and, if possible, what their future plans are. For instance, a whole town can be decimated by just one large employer shifting production elsewhere.

If your customers are solely other businesses, do not be misled into thinking that the stability and prosperity of consumer markets do not matter. After all they, like all businesses, ultimately depend on the consumer for success. Your principal client may not be selling direct to the consumer but the customers they do business with or, failing that, the next business down the chain of distribution will be. The effects of a depression in consumer markets will always filter down the chain of distribution from retailer, through intermediaries to the manufacturer and eventually to their suppliers. Sometimes the delay can be measured in terms of weeks and in others in terms of months or even years, as can be the case with engineering businesses making equipment for major production processes. Of course, the opposite is true when the economy booms – suppliers of plant and equipment to manufacturers will be the last to benefit.

■ What is the current unemployment rate among your customer groups?
■ Who employs your customers?

- What is the state of their (your customers' employers) financial health?
- What are the plans of your customers' employers?
- Are any new employers planning to come into the area? (Contact the Planning Department of your local authority and review the local press to find out.)
- If your customers are other businesses, then it is essential that you check their financial standing. You must watch their markets and marketing closely – after all, you depend on them for success.
- What is the time-lag between boom and slump in your sector and boom and slump in relevant consumer markets?
- What is the scale of the knock-on effect of boom and slump in consumer markets?

■ *Changes in disposable income*

Changes in real disposable income (that is, after discounting the effect of inflation and taking into account taxation) can have a more dramatic effect on some markets than others. To illustrate, between 1981 and 1986, real disposable income rose by 17 per cent. The most notable effects on sales to consumers were increases in clothes (up by 34 per cent) and the purchases of TVs and so on (up by a colossal 97 per cent), whereas the spending on basic needs, such as food, remained fairly static.

Is there any correlation between disposable income and sales in the market you will enter?

■ *Political and legal factors*

- Will changes in legislation in any of the following areas affect your business:
  - product design/safety
  - product description labelling and packaging
  - product guarantees
  - trade practices and regulatory bodies
  - retail trading hours
  - pricing
  - advertising practice.

- Identify the consumer pressure groups that influence your markets. What are their present concerns? What degree of influence do they have on your business' target markets?
- What plans for new housing, commercial, road transport and other developments are in the pipeline that may affect your markets and/or product distribution?
- What subsidies, grants and guidance are available, either to you or your competitors?

■ Population and social factors

The population of the UK has remained fairly static at around 56 million, projected to increase to only 60 million by the year 2025. This, however, masks major changes in the age, sex, economic activity and geographical distribution of the population. For example, a dip in the birth rate in the late 1970s has led to a 25 to 30 per cent reduction in the number of school-leavers in the early 1990s. As a direct result, you would expect the suppliers of educational equipment to suffer, but the same demographic trend will present opportunities for others. For example, the contraction in the youth labour market will encourage women to return to work. The potential result – particularly if the government, via legislation, provides the right financial incentives – is a vast growth in the demand for nursery places.

Scrutinise population trends as they affect your markets. To do this, if relevant, you will need to have demographic features (such as, age, sex, location and so on) of your market included in your customer profile(s). For guidelines on how to construct customer profiles, see Chapter 3.

The ideas and values of a society will affect, to some degree, the actions of all individuals within a social group. They are therefore of concern to all businesses. The trouble is they can be very difficult to pin down and define. None the less, some attempt must be made. Advertisers can make very effective use of changes in mass attitudes and values. Note how effectively the most unlikely businesses have turned 'green'.

- What do you know about your customers' concerns, motivations and attitudes?

- Are any of the following important factors:
  - environmental concerns
  - ethnic or local customs and traditions
  - religious concerns
  - lifestyle aspirations and expectations.

■ Technological factors and change

Developments in technology have enabled businesses to create vast new markets, as has been the case with microwaves, computers, satellite and cable television, CD players and so on. It can also change fundamentally the way the business operates. For example, the advent of electronic point of sale equipment and barcode scanning in the retail industry has meant improved customer service and a reduction in operating costs. The same is the case in other industries. New technology has allowed the businesses that can afford to make the investment in equipment, personnel and training to introduce new production and distribution methods.

- What has been the pattern of change in your type of business in the past ten years?
- Has change been rapid or slow? Is this a trend that is likely to continue in the future?
- Which companies have consistently led the way in product and market innovation? What can you learn from them?
- Will you be able to make the same investment in change as your competitors?
- Can you detect early enough the impact that technological changes might have on your production, distribution and marketing plans?

THE COMPLETED PLAN

If you have thought about your business idea long and hard, and have done some initial research along the lines of the above, you will have prepared the ground for building a detailed plan of action. Although the completed business plan is still a distant goal, it will nevertheless help to map out what has to be achieved. Working through the rest of this book will help you in this quest.

Your business plan (we will consider how it should be formally laid out for a loan application in Chapter 8) can be subdivided in many ways but it must cover the following areas.

■ Sales and marketing

No customers means no business! This simple truth means that you must define your business idea in terms of:

- the customers it will serve;
- why customers will buy from you rather than the competition.

You need to collect as much information as possible about the market for your business. Some of the key questions have already been posed in this chapter and the whole area will be considered in detail in the next two chapters.

The size and demands of your potential market and the activity of your competitors will lay down the parameters for decision making relating to the:

- scale of operation
- location and distribution
- competition
- sales targets
- pricing and overall trading policy
- products and services
- additional customer services that need to be offered
- advertising and sales promotion policies.

In summary, as a small business or SME can only rarely significantly influence and change the nature of the market, you should evolve your overall business idea in response to the threats and opportunities posed by it.

■ Costs

This area of the plan will detail all the costs faced in starting and operating the business for at least the first year's trading. Here, care should be taken not to mistake all business expenditure as cost. Costs relate only to expenditure on those items that are used up in a given period of trading, such as stock sold, pay, electricity, rent, rates, insurance and so on. Expenditure on items often associated with start-up, such as equipment and premises, is not a cost as these things are something you are likely to still have at the end of the trading period and are called assets. As each year goes by, some assets will lose value as a result of ageing and wear and tear. This loss in value is a cost and is known as depreciation.

Some costs, such as electricity, rent and rates, do not change in proportion to how much you sell and so are known as fixed costs or, more commonly, overheads. Other costs, most significantly stock, vary in direct proportion with the amount you sell and so are known as variable or direct costs.

A detailed investigation into the full costs of operating the business cannot be made until decisions relating to the scale and location of the operation (derived in part from market research and financial constraints) are made. However, identification of suppliers can begin almost immediately.

The formulation of objectives in this area are inextricably linked with sales targets and investment decisions.

You need to itemise and justify all costs.

■ Profit

This aspect of your planning will provide one of the acid tests of your sales and cost objectives. Will your sales bring in sufficient revenue to cover all costs and provide you with an 'acceptable profit'?

You will earn profit from the production or buying of merchandise or services and selling them. The difference between the direct or variable costs and the selling price is your gross profit, which will have to contribute to payment of your overheads. What's left over is your net profit.

> *Will your sales bring in sufficient revenue to cover all costs and provide you with an 'acceptable profit'?*

There are several factors that affect total profitability:

- sales volume
- price
- overheads or fixed costs
- gross profit margin.

The term 'margin' needs to be explained. It is the percentage difference between direct costs and sales price. If I sell a machine for £50,000 that cost £20,000 to make, my total gross profit is £30,000. The gross profit margin is 60 per cent.

$$\frac{50,000 - 20,000}{50,000} \times 100 = 60\%$$

Do not make the mistake of assuming that a high gross profit margin will bring high total gross profit. It's the number of times you earn that profit margin which determines the total gross profit earned at the end of the day.

When you have brought together your estimates of costs and revenue, it is likely you will have to make at least minor adjustments to your sales and cost objectives. In fact, the establishment of your sales, cost and profit plans, because they are so closely related, will take place hand in hand.

The key financial projections in this area are the following.

- **Break-even calculation** This is the calculation of the sales level required to cover all costs, both fixed and variable. One important question to answer is 'How long will it take for the business to break even?'
- **Projected profit and loss account** This projection will give the expected position on sales, costs and profits at the end of the first year's trading.

■ Investment and finance

The amount of money you will have to invest in the assets of the business will be determined primarily by:

- the scale of operation;
- whether or not you intend to buy freehold or leasehold;

- the stock levels you will have to carry;
- the level of credit sales.

Any increase in the scale of the operation, the level of credit sales, and a decision to buy freehold will increase your investment in the business. Any decision to rent or lease instead of buying major items of equipment (ranging from vans to electronic tills) will reduce your investment.

Further, most businesses experience peaks and troughs in the amount of money going out (for example, due to quarterly bills all coming at the same time) and coming in (say, due to seasonal fluctuations in sales). Therefore, at times there will be more money going out than coming in. This is fine over a short period of time, but in the long term, you must plan your business so that a cash surplus position is reached. Full instruction, discussion and advice on cash flow forecasting and control is given in Chapter 7.

Finally, the rate of return on the money invested in the business should be in excess of what it would earn in, say, a savings account.

Having established how much is to be invested in the business and when, the right type of finance must be selected, applied for and secured (see Chapter 8). Key projections in this area should include the following.

- **A cash flow forecast** This lists all monies coming in and going out of the business, along with monthly balances. This document is an indispensable planning tool for, as we have discussed, the availability of sufficient cash resources is vital for business survival.
- **Projected balance sheets** The balance sheet lists, for any given point in time, what the business possesses (assets) and how it is financed (liabilities). Two balance sheets are required:
  - **one for start-up** to clearly show what investment is required on day 1 of the business and how it will be used;
  - **one for the end of the first year's trading** to show the business' expected financial health after the first 12 months, which, along with the projected profit and loss account, should substantiate the business' financial objectives.

■ Business organisation and control

Once objectives and plans have been set in marketing and sales, costs, profit, investment and finance, you will need to put into place systems to carry out your plans. You will need systems and policies for:

- maintaining the security of cash and merchandise;
- recording all transactions in the business;
- monitoring sales;
- ordering goods;
- selecting, training and managing staff;
- handling complaints;
- conforming to legislation affecting your business.

SUMMARY

The key reason for failure of small businesses and SMEs is the failure to plan. The mistakes that they make are testimony to this.

How formal you make the planning process is largely up to you, and will depend on the nature and scale of your business. However, you will be well advised to accord with the general planning principles given in this chapter. In particular, you should clearly identify the constraints on your overall business plan and develop objectives to minimise the threats posed and maximise the opportunities presented. In addition, you should now be aware of some of the major areas of concern, the importance of thinking through decisions and how a decision in one area can affect decisions made in others.

The rest of the book, which can be referred to in any order, will take you through the detailed planning you need to do. Careful planning now will:

- **minimise problems and risk;**
- **help prevent you from making potentially ruinous moves;**
- **raise your confidence in your ability to start up and run your business;**

- provide you with a framework that, when your business is up and running, will help you to identify and avoid potential problems before they happen.

Finally, as indicated in the following diagram, planning is not a process that ends when you eventually start your business but one that should continue throughout its life.

Summary of the business planning process

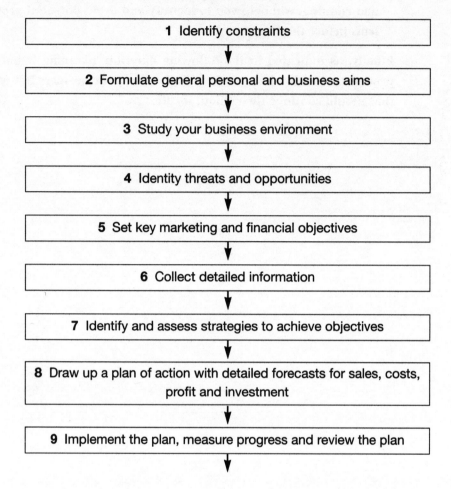

1 Identify constraints

2 Formulate general personal and business aims

3 Study your business environment

4 Identity threats and opportunities

5 Set key marketing and financial objectives

6 Collect detailed information

7 Identify and assess strategies to achieve objectives

8 Draw up a plan of action with detailed forecasts for sales, costs, profit and investment

9 Implement the plan, measure progress and review the plan

The market

INTRODUCTION

In starting to investigate whether or not your business idea is really viable – that is, whether or not it will make an acceptable profit and meet your personal requirements – you will undoubtedly be tempted to start to investigate a range of aspects at the same time – from premises, through legal requirements to what it will cost. True, some initial groundwork should be done in all of the major areas, but little of any meaning can be achieved without some forecast of sales for your first year's trading. For instance, there is no point in looking for premises and researching costs for a large restaurant when the market will only generate trade for a smaller operation. Also, of course, the question as to whether or not the market demands a restaurant in your location is another question to be researched and answered!

> *Refine your business idea and make sure you are offering the right product and/or service to your market, in the right quantity, at the right price, in the right place and at the right time.*

To the lay person, there is much mystery surrounding market research. It is easy to think that it is something only the large companies and professionals do. However, nothing could be further from the truth. Market research is largely common sense; it is about finding out. Much of that finding out can be done by you, the individual businessperson, just as well and in some cases better than by the large 'professional' market research organisation. In any case, their services can run into thousands of pounds!

This chapter is designed to help you research the market for your business. Specifically, your research should help you to:

- refine your business idea and make sure you are offering the right product and/or service to your market, in the right quantity, at the right price, in the right place and at the right time;
- forecast your sales for the start-up period and first year's trading.

To achieve these overall goals, you will need to discover the answers to the following questions.

- Why will people buy my product?

- Who will buy my product?
- How much will my customers buy?
- Who/what is the competition?
- What are their strengths and weaknesses?
- What will my market share be?
- When will my customers buy?
- What price will my customers pay?
- Is my market growing or contracting?

WHAT AM I SELLING – WILL CUSTOMERS BUY?

The commonest response to the first part of the question is to answer in literal terms. For instance, the owner of a small shop might reply, 'What am I selling? That's obvious isn't it? I'm selling groceries, wines and spirits and household goods!' A response such as this is short-sighted and dangerous for a number of reasons.

- Defining your business simply in terms of the products or services it sells puts blinkers on you before you open the doors for business. It is committing the mortal sin of concentrating on what you want to sell rather than on what your customers want to buy.
- A business so blandly described lumps itself with all other businesses of a similar type. Nothing will mark it out as being different from its competitors apart from its drabness!

Therefore, to be successful, there are two simple rules:

- define your business in terms of what your customers want to buy;
- be different from the competition.

Getting the first part right is to understand why people buy. Getting the second part right is a matter of researching the competition, seeing the threats and opportunities (as we did with the wider environment in the last chapter) and building a business that concentrates on your strengths and minimises your weaknesses.

So, what do customers want? The answer is relatively simple. They buy to satisfy some need or desire. The problem, however, is more complicated than most because needs are many and varied, ranging from the basic physical needs of shelter, food and safety essential for survival, through the need to satisfy personal vanity to attainment of intellectual and spiritual satisfaction. It is said that money can't buy you love. Perhaps it can't, but florists, card shops and jewellers can make a good profit helping it along the way. The cosmetics industry sells dreams of beauty, sophistication, youth – its products gratify our egos. People may buy lager to quench their thirsts, but many also buy it because it has an image that appeals and matches to a self-image they aspire to. In each case, the customer is motivated by the benefits – perceived or actual – derived from the purchase rather than the actual purchase itself. The message is:

> **concentrate on what the product can do for the customer, rather than what it is.**

We have learnt that customers buy benefits and not products. However, why is it, where identical products are offered at the same price, some customers will buy from one business while others buy from another? The answer to the question is to be found in your own practical experience as a customer – try the following exercise.

Exercise

List as many of the factors that influenced your decision to buy three recent, but different, products or services as you can. Also, think about where you bought them from and, finally, try to isolate what it was that influenced your choice.

How did you get on? How many times was the decision to buy influenced solely by the benefits attached to the product? I would guess this affected most if not all of your choices, but was not always top of the list. There will have been other reasons. Did the price of the purchase make a major difference or were you attracted by the convenience and availability offered by the place you bought it from; or was the decision more emotional than rational? Perhaps the business' promotion communicated an image or lifestyle that appealed? In the end, it was no doubt a trade-off between the benefits offered by each – your mix of 'wants' matched with the marketing mix of the business from which you eventually made the purchase (as illustrated in Figure 3.1).

Fig. 3.1 To be successful, you must match what you offer to what the customer wants

This concept of a 'marketing mix' provides a framework for you to build a unique selling proposition. The trick is to sell the benefits that are of greatest importance to your customers. You need not meet your competition head on – it is unlikely that you will be able to compete in every area, rather, but, as already noted, you should endeavour to match your strengths with the wants of a particular group of customers.

I will return to the concept of the marketing mix in the next chapter, when you will begin the task of putting together a marketing plan. However, before that task can begin, you need to know as much as possible about your customers and the competition. Also, before we leave this section, it is advisable that you should make a start at defining what you are selling.

My product/service is ....

I will offer ....

Because my customers want ....

....

Select one or more competitors and complete the following for each one.

Competitor's name ....

Their product/service is ....

but they also sell the following package of benefits.

Benefit	Their strength/weakness	My strength/weakness
Product		
Price		
Place		
Promotion		

WHO WILL BUY MY PRODUCT?

In the last section we saw the dangers of defining the business simply in terms of the products it sells. It is equally dangerous to describe your customers in the same terms. Defining customers solely as house buyers, drivers, smokers, machine-tool buyers and so on is fraught with problems. Such an approach totally fails to take into account the wants of the customers concerned. Further, it lumps all users of a particular product together. Without an audit of customer wants and, therefore, any meaningful description of specific customer groups, businesses will attempt to compete only in the areas of price and product and ignore other aspects of the marketing mix.

We can clearly see the potentially disastrous nature of this approach when one considers what is often referred to in business circles as the 80/20 rule. The 80/20 rule or Pareto effect describes the commonly observed phenomenon that about 20 per cent of customers account for around 80 per cent of sales. The task is to identify this group of people and target your efforts and resources on their wants.

■ Finding the target market

Making reasoned guesses about why people may buy from your business should have helped you focus on who those people are. For many products/services, the market can be split up into different groups of customers – that is, different 'market segments'. An often-used analogy is to imagine the market as a large orange – you can peel an orange and separate it into segments. There are many ways, too, of 'segmenting' a market.

■ Age

This is an obvious option when your product, by its nature, is aimed at a specific age group – for example, toys, children's clothes, holidays for the retired and so on. As a general rule, people at different ages have different needs. The retired couple may have a greater need for durability and reliability, while a young couple with a family and a tight budget may have low cost as a priority. Your product may appeal to different age groups for different reasons.

■ Sex

Will your customers be mainly women or men? Again, an obvious criteria if your product, by its nature, is aimed at a specific sex, for example men's or ladies' clothing. However, pause for thought. The purchaser of the product is not always the end-user. For instance, it is well known that many women buy clothes for their husbands, sons and boyfriends.

■ Location

Often, and in particular with any kind of retailing business, you can define your customers by where they live, work and where they go. For instance, a fast food outlet would, ideally, be located near to shops, bingo halls, places of work (to cater for meal breaks and so on), nightclubs and drinking venues, a sports shop next to a sports centre, and so on.

■ Occupation/employment

Research has shown that there are varying degrees of correlation between a person's occupation and tastes/attitudes. Which social class or occupational group image is your product going to appeal to?

■ *Income*

Not many businesses appeal to all ranges of income. Obviously, if your business is going to focus on high-priced quality products, your customers will, more than likely, be in a high-income bracket.

■ *Leisure activities*

With a growing number of people taking early retirement, becoming unemployed, working shorter hours, receiving longer holidays and enjoying better standards of living, the leisure industry is an ever-growing one. You may find it useful to define your customers according to their leisure activities – specifically, as participants in certain sports or in general terms, for example, 'healthy-living types'.

■ *Usage*

A useful way to define your market is to identify segments based on the way your product is used by your customer. On a simple level, heavy use/medium use/low use/or skilled use/unskilled use. For example, a firm producing body filler for cars might find it has a number of different markets based on usage: a frequent low-skill user ('botchers'); a high-skill infrequent user (perfectionists); and a high-skill large-quantity user (trade market). Each of the three markets will have different characteristics and needs. Research might uncover that the low-skill frequent user is the largest market and is predominantly made up of non-manual working, low-income bracket owners of low-value old cars.

 Checklist

Make a first attempt to segment the market for your business using the process (or similar) below.

The product/service is bought on what basis?

1 Frequently as an everyday essential?

2 As a treat or luxury?

3 Most often as a gift?

4 Only bought after long and serious consideration?

5 On the advice of others?

6 Used only by the customer?

7 Often on impulse without much thought?

8 To help the customer enjoy their leisure time?

9 To help the customer enjoy a better lifestyle?

10 To save the customer time and make domestic chores easier and possibly fun?

11 To save the customer money?

12 To solve practical problems?

13 To deal with emergencies?

14 Always for the same purposes/uses?

15 For many different purposes/uses?

16 To help the customer belong to a social group, attain a particular lifestyle or image?

The customers who buy this product/service can be most usefully described by what characteristics?

1 Sex?

2 Age?

3 Marital status, and number of children?

4 Household location?

5 Living accommodation (house, flat, mortgage, rented)?

6 Neighbourhood type?

7 Income?

8 Disposable income (have they got spare cash or are they on a tight budget)?

9 Occupation, unemployed, retired?

10 Education?

11 Membership of clubs and associations?

12 What they do with their leisure time?

13 What they do and where they go to socialise?

14 Participation in sporting activities?

15 Religious activity and beliefs?

16 Ethnic group?

17 Local/regional customs and traditions?

18 Political beliefs?

19 Environmental concerns?

20 Lifestyle aspirations?

■ Industrial and commercial target markets

An often-made mistake is the belief that industrial customers are only motivated by the technical features and price of the product. Certainly, such considerations are important, but are relatively meaningless outside the context of the factors that surround the product's usage and ultimate value to the purchaser.

> *An often-made mistake is the belief that industrial customers are only motivated by the technical features and price of the product.*

It is crucial to identify the relative influence of the user over the purchaser in the decision to buy. Particularly in larger companies, it is often the case that the user and purchaser will operate in different spheres of the company, be constrained in different ways and have to meet different objectives. What decisions will the buyer make when working within a purchasing budget while trying to meet usage specifications from a production engineer?

As customers in industrial markets will be known by name, the best place to start is with a thorough analysis of each. A 'profile' should be compiled for each one. The information contained in each profile will, of course, vary depending on the type of market. Use the following checklist to help you profile industrial and commercial customers.

 Checklist

Customer profile for ....

1 Type of customer's business (for example, manufacturer, wholesaler, retailer, service and so on)?

2 SIC code (Standard Industrial Classification), as applicable. Note that useful information can be gained about activity in each industrial sector by reference to published statistics (see later in this chapter).

3 Number of employees?

4 Sales turnover?

5 Customer's market (note that the demand generated in industrial markets is ultimately derived from consumer markets)?

6 Who presently supplies this potential customer?

7 Products/services normally purchased?

8 Uses to which they are put?

9 User requirements (key benefits sought, translated into key technical features as appropriate)?

10 Importance to the customer of:
   - price
   - quality
   - reliability
   - support services?

11 Typical order size?

12 Frequency of purchase?

13 Geographic location (quantify the cost of distribution if appropriate)?

14 Other considerations?

■ Guidelines for selecting a target market

Whatever characteristics you use to define your target markets, they must be able to pass the following tests.

- Can the segment be measured? Will you be able to estimate the number of customers in each segment? If you have used any kind of demographic (population) characteristics in your market profile – such as age, sex, location and so on – this should be relatively easy (see page 56. 'How much will they buy?) Measuring a segment becomes much more difficult if it is solely defined by a characteristic such as taste in fashion.
- Is the segment of a significant size? To make the point, a target market consisting of two people – unless each represents a large potential revenue earner (that is, a large business customer) – is absurd. None the less, it is possible to become over-enthusiastic and define too many target markets, resulting in confusion.

- Is the segment a potentially profitable one? There is little point in having a large target market that has little ability to purchase your product or service. The definition of market need also includes the ability to pay (see pages 56 and 68, How much will they buy? and What price will they pay?).

- Will you be able to gain access to the segment? It is not enough to know that the segment exists, that it is 'out there somewhere'. It is important that you can reach, communicate and sell to the identified target market. Some markets are effectively cut off from newcomers or at least very difficult to get into. For instance, many central and local government departments have to select from an approved list of suppliers.

Some large companies can provide good business but are notorious as slow payers (usually small businesses and SMEs cannot afford to have their cash tied up in this way). Some segments that are widely scattered geographically present too large a distribution problem (see Chapter 4).

■ Having problems?

If you have found great difficulty in defining your market and its different segments, is it because the description of your business is too vague, narrow or broad? If this is not the reason, is it because you are simply not sure what customer groups, categorised by demographic (income, age, sex and so on), psychological (tastes, interests and so on), geographical and usage characteristics, are seeking the benefits your product potentially offers? If it is the first of the two reasons, then go back to your business ideas and give it more thought. If it is the second, then perhaps you need to approach the problem of market segmentation from a different direction – by first identifying customer groups by specific needs in the general area of your line of business, then shaping your business idea to provide benefits to meet those needs (see page 4, Spotting a gap in the market).

■ Finding out

Even if you have made a good arm-chair analysis of your market seg-ments, you will no doubt want them

> *Observe the competition's customers in some structured way.*

verified. There are various ways of doing this. Here we will consider the use of survey techniques, primarily questionnaires and simple methods of observation, and the use of information in the form of existing surveys and statistics.

If you have made little headway in identifying your market, but feel you have a good business idea, a good starting point is to observe the competition's customers in some structured way. From simple observation, it is possible, depending on the type of business being researched, to deduce the customers' age, sex, time of visit, mode of transport and even the type of purchase made. From the quality and style of clothing and general image, it is also possible to make some subjective stab at their income group.

Careful noting of the benefits the competition offers will also pro-vide a useful guide to who their customers are. Your research can also be enhanced if you serve a simple questionnaire on a sample of the customers to find out more about them.

■ Guidelines for devising questionnaires

- **Don't** make the mistake of starting with the questions without being really clear about what you want to find out. Questions are often written down because they sound good, not because they will find out what the research wants to know. Take some time first to detail exactly what you want to find out. *Have clear objectives*.
- **Include a means of identifying customer groups** by some tangi-ble and measurable factors, such as age, location, occupation, business activity and so on.
- **Keep it short** Otherwise the respondent will become bored and give inaccurate information.
- **Make it clear** Never ask two questions in one. Always test the questionnaire on a small group to see if any questions are mis-

leading, confusing, likely to have two meanings, suggest an answer and so on.

- **Evaluate the effectiveness of each question against objectives before use** When the questionnaire is complete, go over it again and ask of each question, 'Why am I asking this question, what useful information will it give me?' Modify or discard any questions that don't pass this test.

- **Remember, the information collected will later have to be collated and analysed** Therefore, where it is appropriate, give the respondent a range of answers to choose from. This makes it easier to sort the questionnaires after the survey.

When designing questions, it is important to select the right 'types' of questions to elicit the information you require. Let's consider the alternatives.

▓ Yes/no questions

These are closed questions, offering only two responses. For example:

Do you use carbon filters? YES/NO *(please circle)*

This type of question has limited value and should be used sparingly. It is often used at the beginning of the questionnaire to 'qualify' the respondent against the sample criteria.

▓ Multiple choice questions

These are closed questions, but they offer more than two responses. For example:

How many carbon filters do you use each week?
    fewer than 100
    100 to 200
    201 to 300
    301 to 400
    401 to 500
    500 +

The structuring of the responses allows for easy collation of information.

■ *Scale and semantic response questions*

These allow the respondent to exercise some freedom in response. They are useful for obtaining information on attitudes, opinions, motivations, perception and so on. For example:

> How would you rate your present supplier of carbon filters on product quality?
>
> poor .... very good
> *(please mark with a cross the point on the scale that matches your view)*

You could achieve similar ends by asking them to rate the supplier on a scale of say one to five.

You can often elicit responses which reflect attitudes by using an association/projective questioning technique. For example:

> What word or phrase would you associate with:
> Sainsbury ....
> Safeway ....
> Tesco...
> Kwik Save ....

Similarly:

> Please complete the following sentence.
> Manufacturers who use carbon filters ....
> ....

■ *Open-ended questions*

These allow respondents total freedom in the way they can answer. They are often found at the end of a questionnaire. For example:

> Would you like to make any additional points about carbon filters?

Although the responses to these kinds of questions may be difficult to collate and categorise, they may well unearth important information about the product or market that you would remain ignorant of if the open question was not asked.

■ Use the library

Much can be gained from studying existing market research. Some-body may have found the answers for you already, but where do you find them? The starting point and per-haps the most underused resource by businesspeople (considering it is free!) is the reference section of your local public library. Here you will find a wealth of information.

Much can be gained from studying existing market research and published research.

- **Central and local government statistics** These give such infor-mation as family expenditure on different goods and services, population statistics (age, income groups, geographical distribu-tion and so on) (see page 56, How much will they buy?). Some local government offices also publish monthly or quarterly reviews of different sectors of business. Government publications of interest include:
  - *Social Trends*
  - *Family Expenditure Survey*
  - *General Household Surveys*
  - *Economic Trends*
  - *Regional Trends*
  - *Annual/Monthly Digest of Statistics.*

  These are special surveys published by the Social Survey Unit of the Central Office of Information.

  Note: Guides to Government Statistics can be obtained from HMSO bookshops.

- **Directory of business associations**, in larger reference libraries. In this directory you find literally thousands of trade and special interest associations, some of which may be worth contacting to find out if they can help you. Further to this, many trade associa-tions publish periodicals and yearbooks that may also provide useful information. Larger reference libraries also carry trade directories. These contain much information of use to the small business or SME. For example:
  - *Key British Enterprises* gives basic financial information about companies;

- *Kompass* gives a detailed classification of the products and services offered by over 40,000 companies;
- *Kelly's* lists literally tens of thousands of businesses, but gives little information about each company;
- *BRAD (British Rate and Data)* lists advertising rates and audience figures for the main UK newspapers, journals, magazines, TV, radio and other media. In addition, BRAD publishes a *Direct Marketing Directory*, which contains extensive information on companies offering direct marketing services (such as mailing lists).

■ **The marketing, business and social science sections** of the library will also be worth a scan. A search in these sections may reveal some interesting research work relating customer preferences and attitudes to your particular type of business. If you have a university or college library nearby, it is not uncommon to find that members of the teaching staff or students have carried out local research in your area of business. Pay it a visit – most of the hard work could have been done for you!

■ **Market reports** Many organisations publish these. Two of the best-known ones are:
  - MINTEL, which publishes monthly market reports, each report covering a number of consumer markets;
  - KEY NOTE, which publishes market reports on both industrial and consumer markets.
  Specialist publications of possible interest include:
  - *Marketing*
  - *Marketing Week*
  - *Retail Distribution Management*
  - *Industrial Marketing Digest*
  - *Which?*
  - quarterly economic reviews published by the main clearing banks (usually free to customers)
  - *The Economist*.

The prospect of searching through so much 'information' to find what you want can be frightening, like looking for a needle in a haystack. Don't be put off; there is help at hand. Most library assistants are only too pleased to help; they are professionals and know how to track down information. If you approach them in a polite manner, they will usually go to great lengths to find the information for you. However, be prepared to spend the equivalent of a full day at the library and do not be too disappointed if you do not find exactly what you are looking for.

Taking your reasoned guesses about which market segments exist, you can test your idea directly on a sample of each segment and record their reactions. This can be done by use of a questionnaire served personally, by post or telephone; or, better still, if possible, show potential customers a sample of your proposed product/service.

■ Use the Internet

If you don't have an Internet connection, check if your library has Internet access. If not, many further education colleges run short introductory courses on using the Interent and e-mail. Once on-line, you can access a wide range of marketing information and evaluate competitors. (See also Chapter 9.)

HOW MUCH WILL THEY BUY?

This is the really crucial question of how big (in revenue terms) the total market is for your business venture. The answer to the question is inextricably linked to the answers to the following questions.

The more thought you give to selecting the right methods and the more thorough your research, the more accurate your answers are likely to be.

- How many potential customers are there in each segment?
- What quantities will they buy?
- Who/what is the competition?
- What are my competitors' strengths and weaknesses?
- What will be my market share?

As with all market research, there is no way you can guarantee totally reliable and accurate answers to these questions. However, the more thought you give to selecting the right methods and the more thorough your research, the more accurate your answers are likely to be.

■ How many potential customers are in each market segment?

The first step is to attempt to define the catchment area or location of each market segment – if you know where they are, you can count them. You may have done this already in defining each target market. If not, then you must attempt to do this now.

The task of identifying where each segment is located is made easier if it includes some demographic characteristics, such as age, sex, housing, workplace, occupation, transport, and so on. With this information, you can search through central and local government statistics to pinpoint concentrations of the particular characteristics you are looking for. A business selling baby clothes would look for high-population concentrations under the age of five. A property repair business would probably look for high concentrations of 'old' housing stock. Conversely, you can sometimes readily identify the prevalence of the characteristic in the area in which you trade, giving you directly the actual number of potential customers in your trading area.

 Checklist

Are any of your market segments defined wholly or in part by any of the following?

1 Age, sex, occupation, marital status, size of family or place of birth of potential customers.
2 People living in certain types of accommodation.
3 House owners.
4 Students.
5 Unemployed.
6 Owners of hotels.
7 Single parents.
8 Car owners.
9 Owners of more than one car.

10 People living on their own of a certain age.

11 Users of specific types of transport.

12 People living in households above a certain size.

13 People living in households with or without certain amenities.

14 Households with only one adult.

15 Age of a potential customer's house.

If you can define your market segments by any of these characteristics by reference to the *Census County Report* (again, available at your local reference library), you will be able to ascertain the number of potential customers with the required characteristics in your area. The *Census County Report* breaks this information down to local level, so the figures are available for cities, towns and districts. The preceding list is not exhaustive and you are recommended to study your local *Report* at length. If nothing else, you will find the vast array of information on your local area interesting besides being informative.

Some care must be taken when drawing conclusions from all published statistics. With reference to census statistics, these can be anywhere between one and 10 years out of date, so, for instance, the 10,000 children being listed as under 5 years old in 1988 will be buying CDs and teenage fashion in 1998 and will have little use for baby clothes and pushchairs! Mistakes like this are easy to make.

Care must also be taken in estimating the market size in relation to the proposed scale of your business. It would be unrealistic to assume that a whole city or town will represent a potential market for a small retail outlet (unless it was of a highly specialised nature with few competitors). The main catchment area in this case is probably going to be limited to a few miles radius around the proposed location. Therefore, in cases like this, census statistics should be used only as a general indicator. However, as markets covering a small geographic area can be easily surveyed (very accurately) by yourself with the help of your partner or a friend, I suggest the following simple method.

■ *Select a possible location for your business*

- Divide the area up into sections by drawing circles around it at suitable intervals, say one, two, three and four miles, or split the area into housing groups or similar (say, house types, prosperity). You can do both if you wish.
- Compile a questionnaire to identify who will buy, how many will buy, how much and when in each area.
- Select a random sample of say 50 in each section.
- Serve the questionnaire.
- Collate the results by totalling the responses for each section – noting the frequency of any unexpected characteristics that may suggest an alteration in your definition of the target market.
- Express all results as a percentage of the number of question-naires served in each area. For example, convert 20 out of 80 householders within a 1-mile radius who said they would pur-chase from your business at least once a week to 25 per cent ($20/80 \times 100$).
- Identify from your sample who will buy from your business. For example, 80 per cent of all households sampled within a 1-mile radius; 40 per cent of all car owners interviewed; 90 per cent of all businesses with more than 10 employees and so on.
- Carry out a physical count, or informed estimate if this is not prac-tical, of all potential customers with these characteristics.
- Multiply the result by the percentage of positive responses from the questionnaire to obtain the actual size of the potential market for your business. To give a simple example:
  - if, from your sample, 80 per cent of all households interviewed within 1 mile of your proposed site said they will buy from your business once a week; and
  - there are 250 households within 1 mile of your business; then
  - it can be estimated that you will have 200 customers from within 1 mile of your business per week ($250 \times [80/100] = 200$).

  Your research work can be further supported by again referring to businesses similar to your own.

▇ *Find out how much existing businesses are selling*

Go to your local business estate agents and collect details on a number of businesses similar to your proposed venture. These details will usually contain sales figures for the last three years (if they don't, ask for them). Of course, accounts can be inaccurate, but if you take an average of the sales figures for a number of businesses, you should be able to obtain a reasonably accurate figure for that type and size of business.

> *Go to your local business estate agents and collect details on a number of businesses similar to your proposed venture. These details will usually contain sales figures for the last three years.*

If you are planning to start a bigger business, aiming at a larger market or your customers are going to be fairly large businesses, you can obtain valuable information from competitors' or customers' company accounts. By law, limited companies have to file copies of their accounts each year with Companies House, 55 City Road, London EC1Y 1BB. You can see or obtain by post copies of these accounts for a small fee.

▇ *Talk to people in a similar business*

Try to find out what you can by meeting and talking to as many people as possible. For instance, you can view a business as a prospective purchaser and ask pertinent questions about its operation. Sometimes valuable information can be gained from people who work for, rather than own, the business – they perhaps will have less interest in guarding the business' secrets. Also, talk to members of the local trade association (you will find the number in your local telephone directory).

▇ *Review published statistics*

In particular, the state-produced *Business Monitors* (available at your local reference library) cover the main business sectors. These contain a great variety of information, but, importantly, give data such as profits, sales and costs by type and size of business. Obviously, if you can identify your category of business in one of the *Monitors*, you can obtain an indication of the size of market you can expect. However, treat this as an indication only – it must be backed up by further research.

■ What quantities will they buy?

Having identified your target markets and the number of actual customers they will produce, you will need to establish their purchasing power. To know how many customers are in each target market is not the same as knowing how much they will buy. The purchasing power of any given market is the result of the actual number of customers multiplied by their expenditure in that market in a given time period. Although you may have gone some way to establishing the purchasing power of your target markets, by virtue of the fact that many of the questions about the market for your business are interrelated, you will find the further methods introduced here will help you to determine your potential customers' expenditure on the products/services you intend to sell.

> *Knowing the purchasing power for your market is one thing, but estimating your potential share of it is another.*

If your market consists of consumers (that is, the general public) rather than business customers, then an excellent source of information to establish purchasing power is the state-produced *Family Expenditure Surveys (FES)* available at a central reference library. These show in great detail the income and expenditure by type of household of a comprehensive range of consumer goods and services. The information is available for the UK, includes a number of regional analyses, and is published each year.

Note of caution: When calculating approximations of market purchasing power using statistics compiled for larger areas than your envisaged market, you should always attempt to use an alternative method to verify the results. Your local area may be wholly untypical of regional and national spending patterns/trends. Does average household expenditure for your market segments as quoted in the *FES* roughly correspond to information you have derived from other market research sources/techniques? If not, why not? What are the reasons? Which is the more reliable source?

WHO/WHAT IS THE COMPETITION – WHAT WILL BE MY MARKET SHARE?

Knowing the purchasing power for your market is one thing, but estimating your potential share of it is another. In practically all cases, markets are shared with competitors. You must now attempt to find out as much as you can about your competition.

In the preceding sections, mention has been made of the need to look at the competition to help shape your business and identify its markets. Hopefully, therefore, you will have already gone some way towards:

- noting who your competitors are and where they are located;
- identifying how they meet their customers' needs (the benefits they provide) and how well they do it.

You will need to know as much as you accurately can about each competitor's prices, turnover, profitability, product/service range, specific details (specifications and so on of their main products/services), selling methods and so on. Moreover, you will need to compare the strengths and weaknesses of the competition with your business. It is best if you have some structured way of doing this.

First, take an overview of how well the shape of your envisaged business venture is going to match up to your potential customers' needs. This will force you to identify and profile your business' strengths and weaknesses in relation to your envisaged market. Complete the profile in Figure 3.2 for your business. As a guide, the features/attributes important to your customers may include colour, taste, smell, quality, ease of use, presentation and appearance, delivery, opening times, payment terms and price. When you have scored each attribute, join up the respective ratings with a pencil line to obtain two clear profiles, one for customer preferences, one for the strengths and weaknesses of your business.

Try to be as objective and consistent as you can – avoid the temptation to pretend your business idea is other than it is.

Here, list the features/attributes that potential customers will be looking for in your type of business/product service	Score how important each attribute is to your customers	Score your product/service on each attribute
	1 2 3 4 5	1 2 3 4 5
	1 2 3 4 5	1 2 3 4 5
	1 2 3 4 5	1 2 3 4 5
	1 2 3 4 5	1 2 3 4 5
	1 2 3 4 5	1 2 3 4 5

Fig. 3.2 Customer profile

You can, of course, compile a more detailed analysis by extending and modifying the profile to suit your particular business. Further, it is a good idea to compile a number of profiles – one for each of your major market segments. This will enable you to clearly see:

- which market segment you satisfy best;
- which market segment you satisfy better than the competition.

If you can identify a market segment where you are strong in both of these two areas, you are likely to take a larger share of this market away from the competition than otherwise would be the case. (How you would actually go about capturing that larger market share is to be found in Chapter 4.)

Using similar formats (Figures 3.3 and 3.4) to the one you have just used, analyse the threats (their strengths) and opportunities (their weaknesses) your competition presents.

■ Competitor profile, method 1

The first method shown follows the same procedure used to assess your business in relation to its market. It has the advantages of being fairly simple to compile and shows the results in a clear graphic form. Each profile is totalled to provide a single set of figures to make overall comparisons between competitors, your business and each competitor, and your business and the strength of the overall competition.

The second method's (Figure 3.4) advantage over the first is that it takes into account the relative importance of each feature to the market. It is slightly more complicated to construct but should provide more accurate results. Use both methods and compare the results.

Features	Your business	Competitor	Competitor	Competitor	Average score of competition
	1 2 3 4 5	1 2 3 4 5	1 2 3 4 5	1 2 3 4 5	1 2 3 4 5
	1 2 3 4 5	1 2 3 4 5	1 2 3 4 5	1 2 3 4 5	1 2 3 4 5
	1 2 3 4 5	1 2 3 4 5	1 2 3 4 5	1 2 3 4 5	1 2 3 4 5
	1 2 3 4 5	1 2 3 4 5	1 2 3 4 5	1 2 3 4 5	1 2 3 4 5
	1 2 3 4 5	1 2 3 4 5	1 2 3 4 5	1 2 3 4 5	1 2 3 4 5
	1 2 3 4 5	1 2 3 4 5	1 2 3 4 5	1 2 3 4 5	1 2 3 4 5
	1 2 3 4 5	1 2 3 4 5	1 2 3 4 5	1 2 3 4 5	1 2 3 4 5
Totals					

Fig. 3.3 Competitor profile, method 1

■ *Competitor profile, method 2*

- Give each feature a weighting from 1 to 5 to signify its importance to the market segment.
- Award points – on a scale of 1 to 5 – to each business, including your own, on how strong they are in each area.
- Multiply the importance weighting by the points awarded for each business to obtain its score.
- Finally, total each business' score and analyse the results.

Features	Importance	Your business		Competior		Competitor	
		Points	Score	Points	Score	Points	Score
		Totals					

Fig. 3.4 Competitor profile, method 2

■ Calculating the market share – your ability to compete with your competitors to appeal to customers' buying motives

It is possible to estimate your market share using the results of your assessment of the strengths and of the competition in satisfying the market. The principle is based on the assumption that you will capture a market share that is equal or in proportion to your ability to satisfy that market. For example, if the results of your analysis (regardless of which method is used) revealed the following total scores:

Your business	30
Competitor 1	10
Competitor 2	40
Competitor 3	30
Competitor 4	20
Total	130

then it could be estimated that your business has the potential to capture 23.1 per cent of the market, based on its ability in relation to its competitors' to satisfy that market – to appeal to customers' buying motives. If total market expenditure is currently £3000 per week, you will therefore expect to achieve a turnover of £693 per week. To put it another way, there is probably potential for you to gain three times the market share of competitor 1, but only three quarters of the turnover of competitor 2, and so on.

Unfortunately, there is no mathematical certainty about this method. However, it is much better than taking a stab in the dark. Its accuracy will depend on the following factors:

- how accurate you have been in identifying and ranking the need (buying motives) of your potential customers;
- how accurate you have been in your assessment of your business and its competitors;
- how sensitive market share is to customer preferences.

	Score	Share (%)	In £s
Your business	30	23.1	693
Competitor 1	10	7.7	231
Competitor 2	40	30.7	921
Competitor 3	30	23.1	693
Competitor 4	20	15.4	462
Totals	130	100.00	3,000

Calculating the market share for your business on its proportionate ability, in relation to its competitors, to satisfy customer need.

Total purchasing power of the market: £3000 per week.

Fig 3.5 Estimating market share

Exercise To build up a clearer picture of the market, display your results in a table similar to that shown in Figure 3.5. Compare the results to estimates of market shares obtained from some other source. Do they differ markedly? If so, why? Which do you think is the most reliable? Why? Should you err on the side of caution and take the lower of the two estimates for your business?

■ Calculating your initial market share

It is unlikely that from the start-up of your business you will do better than any of your competitors. Therefore, your initial maximum market share will be no greater than:

$$\frac{\text{Total purchasing power (expenditure) of the targeted market}}{\text{Number of competitors plus 1 (your business)}}$$

In the example shown in Figure 3.5, the initial weekly market share would be:

$$\frac{£3000}{5} = £600$$

In most cases, initial trading in the first few months would probably be well below this figure. Research has shown that most businesses take between 6 and 12 months to achieve their expected sales target. After three to six months, if your trading strategies are effective, you can expect to increase your market share in line with your ability to appeal to customers' buying motives.

■ When will they buy?

No matter how good your projections of what your average weekly takings or first year's sales will be, they will be of little real value if you do not know exactly when these sales will occur. Knowing what pattern of sales you will have is crucial for a number of reasons, primarily so you can plan:

- your cash requirements (see Chapter 7);
- to supply the right goods/services at the right time;
- your stock levels;
- your staffing requirements;
- your opening times;
- your sales promotion plan/campaign (see Chapter 4).

It is extremely unlikely your business will have the same sales each and every week. Both the types of products and services sold and the volume in which they are sold can vary quite considerably over dif-

ferent time periods. Extreme examples are toys at Christmas, fire-
works around 5 November and 4 July and, fresh produce with the
seasons. Smaller time variations in demand are of no lesser importance to business planning. The generally recognised fact that most
people do their shopping towards the end of the week has obvious
implications for staffing levels on different days. The pattern of
demand for your particular product or service can be ascertained by
using a number of different sources, some of which were considered
earlier in this chapter:

- General seasonal changes in demand in broad product/service
  groups on a national scale can be identified by using government
  statistics. You will easily find a table giving seasonal variation in
  consumer expenditure on broad product/service groups in a current copy of the *Digest of Statistics*. From the relevant *Business
  Monitors*, you will be able to gather more detailed information.
- If you will be purchasing stock from wholesalers or manufacturers, they will be able to supply you with detailed information on
  patterns of demand for their goods from their sales records and
  years of experience in that sector of business.
- Again, trade and business associations will be able to provide
  information from the wealth of experience of their individual
  members.
- The inclusion of this goal in all your market research techniques,
  customer questionnaires and so on will provide valuable information.
- Ultimately, as your business starts up and progresses, your own
  well-kept sales records will supply you with most of the information you need.

■ What price will they pay?

It is a pity that most small businesses regard competitive pricing as
the main key to generating sales and profit. However, it is only one
factor among many that affects customers' buying decisions – the
examination of why people buy certain products and services has
revealed that much. This doesn't dispute the fact that price is a very

important means of communication between your business and its potential customers; and it is a significant part of your marketing/sales promotion strategy. It means you don't nec-

It is a pity that most small businesses regard competitive pricing as the main key to generating sales and profit.

essarily have to make your product cheap to attract customers.

Certainly low price may be the most important buying motive in relation to some products/services, but not in all cases. For instance, it is commonly known that in the case of high-quality products and services, a low price can have an inverse effect on sales. This is because a low price will force the customer to question the quality of the product or service – 'Why is it so cheap?' The lesson to be learnt is that all your marketing messages should be consistent with one another – a subject we will return to in Chapter 4.

The price at which products and services sell is a prime financial consideration as well. Too low a price and you may fail to make an acceptable profit, no matter what level of sales you achieve; too high a price and you may fail to generate a viable level of sales.

So, how do you decide on what price to charge? Like all aspects of planning for your business, your decision must be based on sound goals. The overall goal behind long-term pricing decisions should be to maximise profits by putting into effect pricing policies that will result in the best combination of sales volume, price and costs, while at the same time conforming to the business' overall image. How to achieve this optimum combination is partly the subject of another chapter (see Chapter 6). However, I would not wish this to mask the importance of the subtle use of price to achieve a number of short-term goals, which are

- **to increase sales volume** Typically, short-term price reductions to help build the business – obviously there will be a cost element to this.
- **to obtain differential pricing/profit maximisation** Often, different pricing policies can be adopted for different target markets – of which two of the many well-known examples are cheap tickets on off-peak period travel and different telephone tariffs for business and commercial users. There is the potential for implementing

different pricing structures/policies where target markets are sufficiently dissimilar and either sympathetic to such a policy – as in the case of price reductions for senior citizens – or unaware of the policy – as in the case where target markets are geographically widely dispersed. At all costs, where such a policy is implemented, profitable customer groups should not be antagonised by such a strategy.

■ **to maximise unit profit** This is where target markets are selected mainly on the basis of their willingness to pay high prices. Physical volume is sacrificed to obtain a high unit profit on each sale.

■ **to protect the business from new competitors entering the market** The business may adopt a short-term pricing policy which reduces profits but makes it difficult for a new company threatening to come into the market to gain a foothold.

Many new businesses will take the lead from their competitors, letting them set the price. The main golden rule not to break when starting up is to ensure that you do not set your prices too low. You can always reduce prices but to raise them is more difficult!

SUMMARY

The importance of establishing a complete profile of your potential market cannot be overstated. Without such detailed information, it is meaningless to attempt to cost the project and establish profitability. Also, the size and nature of the market will dictate the resources your business needs and therefore, the nature and size of the overall investment.

Identifying the characteristics of your target markets, including their potential size, is one thing; converting them into actual sales is another. It is to this task that our attention turns in the next chapter, where you will use the information gained from your research to put together a detailed marketing plan for your business.

✓ Checklist

The plan

1 What are your marketing research objectives?

2 What techniques/methods are you going to use to research the information?

3 Are they valid (will they find out what you want)?

4 Are they reliable?

5 How will you attempt to verify the results?

6 How will you use the results to modify your business idea?

The questions

1 Why will people or businesses buy your product?

2 Who are your potential customers?

3 Who is the end user?

4 Who makes the decision to buy?

5 Where are your potential customers?

6 How much will they buy?

7 How often will they buy?

8 What will they use the product or service for?

9 What are their major needs?

10 Do they control their buying behaviour?

11 How many different customer groups (market segments) can you identify?

12 What is the size of each market segment in revenue terms?

13 Per year, per month, per week, per ...?

14 What will be your market share?

15 How important is price to each market segment?

16 What package of benefits will each segment be looking for?

17 Is the market growing or contracting?

18 What method of distribution (selling method) does the market suggest?

19 What business image does the market most favourably react to?

20 How much will you earn from sales and when in your first year's trading?

The techniques available

1 Questionnaire – what will be its objectives?

2 How will it be implemented (telephone, door-to-door)?

3 What are the characteristics of the sample interviewed?

4 Have you made sure that the sample has the same characteristics as your envisaged target market?

5 How will you make sense of the information collected?

6 Will you use some method of observation (say, customer count)?

7 Have you identified the competition?

8 What have you learned from detailed observation of the competition?

9 Have you collected trading figures for similar businesses that are for sale in the area?

10 Have you checked out the usefulness of the statistics on population and consumer expenditure?

11 Have you spoken to any local businesspeople?

12 Have you checked and read any trade publications in your area of business?

Selling to your customers

1
2
3
4
5
6
7
8
9
10

A framework for a marketing plan – the marketing mix

Product and service decisions • Pricing decisions

Place and distribution decisions

Methods of distribution

Promotion and advertising plans

What do you want to happen? • Making the sale

Summary

A FRAMEWORK FOR A MARKETING PLAN –
THE MARKETING MIX

The methods presented in Chapter 3 should have helped you identify viable market segments in some detail. You will now need a
practical plan to enable you to capture a worthwhile share of those
markets. You can start to build the framework for such a plan by
asking four basic questions about getting potential customers to buy
your product or service in sufficient numbers.

- What benefits will my product or service have to offer potential
  customers?
- What price is the product or service going to be offered at and
  how important is price in influencing potential customers' buying
  motives?
- How is the product or service going to be sold? From what place
  or by what means?
- How is the launch of my business going to be promoted/publi-
  cised to its market segments?

Satisfactory answers to these questions will provide a recipe for ensur-
ing potential customers are turned
into actual customers. The recipe is a well-known one, and is often
referred to as the marketing mix or the four Ps.

> *The benefits the product offers
> must fulfil the needs of your
> customers – otherwise why should
> they buy your product or service?*

- **Product** The benefits the product offers must fulfil the needs of
  your customers – otherwise why should they buy your product or
  service?
- **Price** Your customers may need your product or service, but can
  they afford it?
- **Place** Your product must be sold in a location that is both accessible and attractive to your customers. Such a place, depending
  on the nature of your market, may range from a shop in the city
  centre to individual customers' homes. The way the product is
  sold is also an important consideration.

■ **Promotion** There is little point in getting the product, price and place right if your customers don't know you exist. The right advertising is certainly important, but is not the only factor in sales promotion as will be seen later.

Let's consider each factor or variable in the marketing mix in more detail.

PRODUCT AND SERVICE DECISIONS

Whatever you are selling – whether it be groceries, a haircut, general domestic repairs, washing machines or even something seemingly as simple as bricks – getting the product or service right is a matter of thinking about what it does rather than what it is.

■ what are the features of your business, product or service?

■ what will they do for a potential customer?

■ will the customer need what you are offering?

Listing the features of your product or service provides a detailed breakdown of what it is. For instance, the features of a microwave oven might include 'a pre-programmable timer' and 'available in a range of colours'. Identifying what these features can do for the customer itemises the benefits of buying and using such a product. For the microwave, the following might be true.

Features	*Benefits*
– Pre-programmable timer	– Will cook your meal for you even when you are not at home
– Available in a range of colours	– Can be matched to most kitchen colour schemes

Whether or not the customers will buy depends partly on whether what is being offered is what they want. If the following is true, then the microwave has a good chance of selling.

Features	*Benefits*	*Needs of the market segment*
– Pre-programmable timer	– Will cook your meal for you even when you are not at home	– Working, lead busy lives – have little time to prepare and cook meals
– Available in a range of 'modern' colours	– Can be matched to most kitchen colour schemes	– High-income 'sophisticated' group. Place importance on appearance – need to keep up with trends – likely to have spent a lot of time and money selecting kitchen layout and colours

■ Identifying product benefits

To do this:

- list the features of each of your products;
- for each feature, identify what it may do for, or mean to, the customer;
- every time you think of a feature of a product or some aspect of your business, practise using the phrase 'which means that ...', such as:

The casing is made from carbon fibre, which means that ... less time will be spent on maintenance.

Ten more units can be carried per truck load, which means that transportation costs are substantially reduced.

Longer equipment life, which means that the product has higher resale value and reduced depreciation costs.

The car runs on lead-free petrol and has a catalytic converter, which means that

... the car will run on cheaper petrol,

... less damage will be done to the environment,

... the car meets import regulations.

As you can see, a single feature may offer several benefits. It is important to list them all, for just as a need may be satisfied in many different ways a product may be bought for many different reasons.

Without a thorough features–benefits analysis of your products and/or services it is foolhardy to attempt to make plans in other aspects of the marketing mix. This is because, first, the major determinant of the price a customer will pay is their perception of the product in terms of 'value for money'. It should be obvious that the more benefits a product or service provides that the customer wants, then the greater its 'value for money' factor will be at a given price. Second, a selling message – whether it be in an advertisement or part of a personal selling pitch – depends on isolating what the customer will want to buy.

Your work in the previous chapter should have provided you with ample information to complete a detailed features–benefits and customers' needs card for each main product or service you sell (see Figure 4.1).

Features	Benefits	Customers needs
What it is	What it will do	Is that what the customer needs?

Fig. 4.1   Features–benefits and customers' needs analysis chart

Armed with this information and detailed knowledge of the features of the product/service you are intending to sell, you can use the chart shown in Figure 4.1 to see if you have got it right.

■ Deciding on the type and level of customer service

As the customer's decision to purchase often hinges on the services offered with the product, it is essential that you know:

- the type and level of customer service that is required by customers;
- how your intended provision compares to that offered by the competition;
- the cost of the proposed level of provision.

Service competition offer	Importance to the customer	Cost estimate	Level of service planned
Free trials			
Samples			
Demonstrations			
Brochures/sales literature			
Design service/ pre-sale advice consultancy			
Estimates and quotations			
Customer entertainment			
Credit facilities			
Personal service			
Location/place services – customer care facilities provided			
Stock availability			
Stock range			
Trade-in options			
Delivery (time) (quantity) (frequency)			
Sale or return options			

Service competition offer	Importance to the customer	Cost estimate	Level of service planned
Discounts			
Technical support			
Spares and replacement stock			
Warranty/ guarantees			
On-site service			
After-sales calls			
Training/ guidance in product use			
Product use information			
Complaints handling service			

PRICING DECISIONS

Chapters 3 and 6 deal at length with the subject of price. What needs to be stated here is that it is often a falsehood to consider price as the single most important customer buying motive. You would be well advised to re-read What price will they pay? (Chapter 3) and then complete the following checklist activities.

✓ Checklist

1 For your main products/services, find out and list the current prices being charged by your leading competitors.

Product/service	Your price	Competitor					
		A	B	C	D	E	F
1							
2							
3							
4							
5							

You may find that the price difference between competitors may vary from one product to another. What is the 'difference' when all the major products are considered together?

2 Is there an accepted 'market price' that the majority of the competition adheres to?

3 How sensitive do you expect your sales volume to be to changes in price?

4 What pricing policy are you going to adopt?

Accept the market price, because:
- your costs will not allow you to charge a lower price?
- you can't afford a price war?
- other?

Charge a higher price than the competition, achieve a higher gross profit on each sale while accepting a lower sales volume, because:
- you are in the rare and fortunate position that demand for the product outstrips supply?
- price is not a significant factor in affecting your customers' decision to buy?
- other factors such as quality, personal service, reliability are paramount and overriding factors affecting your customers' decision to buy?
- you have limited production/selling capacity/space available and are faced with a healthy demand for your product?

Charge a lower price than the competition, risk a 'price war', hope that a lower gross profit on each sale will be offset by increased sales, because:

- low prices are singly important to your customers?
- your unit gross profit at market prices is high so you can afford a price war?
- You have low overheads and your competition doesn't?
- it is the only way you will make inroads into the market?
- you have sufficient capital resources to overcome the possible cash problems that can ensue from such action?

Charge different prices to different market segments, because:
- your target markets are sufficiently dissimilar?
- your target markets are separated by time or space?
- your target markets are sympathetic to such a move?
- your product or service is such that it can be offered in different ways and forms to different market segments?

PLACE AND DISTRIBUTION DECISIONS

This is the question of not just where but how (including at what time of the day, week or year) the product will be offered for sale. The place and the method chosen to sell a product or service, along with the product/service itself, add up to a total package of benefits offered to the customer. Most people, for example, are aware that the continued success of the small convenience store is based on benefits to the customer of place and time rather than on the individual benefits of each product it sells. The bread, milk, headache pills and toilet rolls you buy from your local convenience store at 9.30 pm on a Sunday night might be exactly the same products you can buy at a lower price from the supermarket the next morning, but when the total package of benefits, including those to the customer stemming from such facts as opening times and accessibility, are considered along with the actual product or service, it can easily be seen that the two businesses, in catering for different markets, are not 'selling' the same 'product'.

In Chapter 5, we will examine the importance of, and factors affecting, your choice of location, and from the first pages of this book I have stressed the importance of knowing what you are selling. The application of the market research techniques in Chapter 3 is important. Specifically:

- 'When will they buy?' will tell you when you should open and when you should stock and promote certain products/services;
- 'Why will they buy?' – will identify the package of benefits your market segments will be seeking;
- 'Who will buy my product/service?' – will help you decide on a suitable location.

Now you must consider the range of methods for getting your product to the customer.

METHODS OF DISTRIBUTION

Businesses use a range of different means to get their product/service to the customer. Obviously, it is important that you choose a means of distribution that is right for your market while at the same time being aware of alternatives that might gain you access to further markets. Let us look at an example to see what factors need to be considered.

Andrea and Sarah plan to go into business selling fashionable children's clothes. As a result of Sarah's experience as a buyer for a large retail group, they have identified good suppliers and are looking for a suitable method of distribution.

Their first thoughts are to buy a small lock-up shop, but this soon becomes a non-starter when they consider the limited finance available to them. So, they are forced to look at the alternatives. Andrea is on a 'starting your own business' course at the local college and has a list of the major channels of distribution. They both sit down to study it with the hope of coming up with the answer for their particular business.

■ Retail outlet

This general term covers everything from the market stall to large department stores and hypermarkets. The main advantages and disadvantages of selling through your own retail outlet can be summarised as follows.

Advantages

- Enables your business to be easily identified by your customers.
- Can be chosen to be in proximity to concentrations of your customers.
- Can draw on passing trade.
- The business can be more easily controlled and promoted.

Disadvantages

- Can result in high capital costs.
- It is not flexible to some changes that may take place in the market. For example, the neighbourhood can go into decline, parking restrictions might be imposed, your market can 'move away' and so on.

■ Wholesale outlets

These perform the function of holding large volumes of stock, mainly for small retailers. The advantage to the retailer of dealing with a wholesaler rather than the manufacturer is that large chunks of working capital do not have to be tied up in stock. Conversely, the manufacturers prefer to deal with wholesalers instead of small retailers because they are in a position to make bulk purchases. This reduces administration and physical distribution problems and, thus, costs for the manufacturer.

As a new small business, it is unlikely that you will be able to convince a wholesaler to buy in large quantities of your untried product. However, the chief advantage of dealing with a wholesaler is that the costs involved in marketing the product direct to the consumer are taken over by the wholesaler. Obviously, your profit margin will be reduced, but this should be offset by the increase in sales volume and decrease in overheads that occur as a result of using this method.

The main problem with this form of distribution is that you can lose control of the way the product is marketed to the final purchaser. As the level of demand set by the end purchaser will ultimately affect your sales, bad distribution by the wholesaler and poor selling practices by the retailers they sell to can have disastrous effects on your business. The same is, of course, partly true if you intend to set up as a wholesaler yourself.

You can, of course, bypass the wholesaler and sell direct to retailers. You will encounter some of the problems associated with selling to wholesalers, but have the advantage of vetting each retailer in turn. To encourage retailers to give selling space to your product, you might consider offering:

■ sale or return terms;
■ in-store merchandising – a service where you will go into their shops, help the retailer make the order, stock their fixture and, in addition, possibly supply display stands and promotional material (this makes you a more attractive proposition to the retailer while, at the same time, allowing you to retain some control over the way the product is marketed to the final purchaser).

■ Mail order

This is an increasingly popular method of distribution. It involves direct selling to customers via such mediums as TV, radio and press advertising. In most cases, the customer is encouraged to place an order using an order form attached to the advertisement.

The attraction of this method for the new small business is in the fact that costly premises don't have to be acquired. However, the real advantages of this method are that it can be used to:

■ reach and distribute to a market that is geographically scattered;
■ reach a wide range of market segments by choosing different advertising mediums and approaches;
■ allow the business to engage in differential pricing policies between market segments;
■ adapt quickly to changes in the market.

Further, a small business using this method does not necessarily have to buy in large quantities of stock in advance of sales. In many cases, stock need only be purchased when orders and payment are received. This has the obvious advantage of greatly reducing working as well as fixed capital requirements (see Chapter 7).

There are certain disadvantages with this method, which are, chiefly:

- advertising and sales promotion costs will be relatively high when compared to other methods;
- many less than honest traders have used this method and given it bad publicity;
- many products/services do not lend themselves to this impersonal method of selling.

■ Door-to-door selling

This is the method of distribution that everybody makes jokes about! Its popularity is on the decline, but it can and should still be considered as a possibility. The main problem is getting over the consumer's basic distrust of this method and the time involved in making each sale.

■ Party plan selling

This is another low-cost method of distribution that has gained popularity, particularly in the USA. Usually a company will engage agents who will organise 'parties' in their own homes, demonstrating and selling the company's products to their friends and relatives. The agent is usually paid on a commission basis and encourages customers to become agents themselves. This method can work well if carefully organised. However, the problem is its own popularity – the marketplace is becoming overrun with 'party plans'. For the small business, 'party plan' offers similar advantages to mail order.

■ Deciding which method is best for your business

After studying the various methods of distribution open to them, and much discussion, Andrea and Sarah decide to market the children's clothes initially via a party plan arrangement. Their reasons are as follows.

- **The needs of the market** The purchasers of their product would be young mothers who may not be able to 'get out of the house'. They may also appreciate the opportunity to socialise with other young women in the same situation as themselves. So, party plan seemed the method that might appeal to the market the most.

- **Capital considerations** Using party plan, only a range of samples would need to be purchased. Stock would only be acquired as orders were placed (remember, Sarah had identified suppliers who could be relied on). Also, there would be no need to raise capital for premises.
- **Financial considerations** Although transport costs would be high because of the need to make frequent visits to wholesalers, over-heads should be low. As agents would be paid on a commission only basis, labour costs would vary in proportion with sales.

Keeping an eye on the future, Andrea and Sarah decide that when they have built a sound base from party plan sales they will venture into mail order. The plan is to build up enough capital from these two methods to open a small retail outlet.

Did they make the right decision? Well, 18 months on, Andrea and Sarah have 12 party plan agents and steady sales from that aspect of the business. Their venture into mail order has been something of a disaster as they have found that the promotional costs far outweigh the profits from the volume of business they have brought in. They still haven't got enough capital for the shop, but have managed to start a relatively successful market stall.

What methods of distribution are you going to use to help sell your product/service? Use the following checklist to help you come to a decision.

 Checklist

1 Will it meet the needs of your market segments?
2 Will it be compatible/complementary with/to other elements of your marketing mix?
3 Will it produce sufficient sales?
4 What are the working and fixed capital requirements of such a method?
5 What costs will it involve?
6 Will the method allow you to charge a price that will give you a sufficient profit margin?
7 What methods do your competitors use? Are these the right ones?

8   Will the method preclude you from controlling the way the product or service is marketed to the end purchaser? How important is this to your business?

PROMOTION AND ADVERTISING PLANS

The final part of your marketing plan is the promotion of the product/service package. The first objective of any business' promotion plan is to tell potential customers of its existence. The second is to get them to visit it. The third is to get them to buy. The fourth is to get them to come back. This section will therefore deal with the method and means of doing this. Your overall objective is to turn the people who make up your potential target markets into loyal customers.

■ Developing a sales promotion plan

There are several key aspects to developing a sales promotion plan.

- What do you want to happen (specifically)?
- What message will make it happen (what message will be sent, how can it be made persuasive)?
- What media will be used to communicate the message?
- What will it cost?
- What profits will it generate?
- How can you find out if the sales promotion worked?

Exercise   If you have done a good job in answering the questions posed in Chapter 3 and this chapter, you should be in a fairly good position to summarise the information by answering the following two broad questions.

- *What image will your business attempt to project?* This should be built on and from the package of benefits you are offering to your customers.
- *By what means can potential customers be attracted away from the competitors?* By this stage you should have carried out a detailed analysis of the competition, as suggested in this chapter and in more detail in Chapter 3.

This summary will provide you with the message you wish to send to your potential customers.

WHAT DO YOU WANT TO HAPPEN?

What do you want your potential customers to do?

Deciding on the message you wish to send to your customers is not as easy as it first appears. First, you must decide what you want them to do and, second, what will have to be in the message to persuade them to do what you want.

What do you want your potential customers to do?

What you want them to do is really your set of specific objective(s) for the sales promotion. To help you promote your business start-up, in response to the message you send, do you want your customers to:

- note you exist?
- visit your premises?
- make requests for further information?
- make an order?
- other?

■ How are you going to make it happen?

Next, how are you going to persuade your potential customers to respond in a positive manner to the message? As I have stressed throughout, for products and services to sell, they have to have genuine benefits for potential customers. Therefore, your best chance of getting potential customers to do what you

How are you going to persuade your potential customers to respond in a positive manner to the message?

want is to point out the benefits of becoming one of your customers. To do this you need to stress more than just the benefits of the actual product or service being offered for sale. The customer services offered by the business must also be stressed, as in the earlier example of the convenience store, the actual product did not contain the key selling points – it was the opening times and accessibility of the store to its customers that were the appealing benefits.

This persuasive message, once identified, should become the basis for building an image, something you become known for, such as:

- friendly, personal service;
- speed and reliability of delivery;
- excellent after-sales service and back-up.

This should be promoted at all times. Good advertisements and sales promotions should follow what has now become commonly known as the AIDA formula. For an advertisement to have a chance of success, it must attract customers' **a**ttention, gain their **i**nterest that, in turn through the message being communicated, generates **d**esire to take the **a**ction of going out and buying the product.

- **Attention** Most prospective customers scan over poor advertisements without paying attention. You need to stop this browsing with something that will focus their minds. Clever use of graphics, colours or bold headlines can sometimes achieve this.
- **Interest** The next step is to gain their attention long enough to transmit the central message. Concentrate on trying to relate to what your research has identified as your customers' most important needs. Try to do it in a simple but interesting way. Don't make the mistake of making the advertisement confusing and boring by trying to communicate too much – keep to the most powerful messages.
- **Desire** If you have managed to capture their attention long enough and the message is powerful enough, then the potential customer should feel the need to purchase the product.
- **Action** Finally, the advertisement should include some aspect that will encourage the customer to come to you and make the purchase. Many advertisements seek to do this by using such phrases as 'limited offer', 'while stocks last', 'free trial', and so on. Others offer money off coupons or make suggestions such as 'come down next week on our late opening night' (including simple directions for how to get there) or encourage the potential customer to give them a telephone call straight after seeing or hearing the advertisement. In fact, any ploy can and should be used (as long as it is legal and honest) to instil action in the customer.

Checklist

1 Be clear about the objectives for the 'copy'.

2 Define the target audience.

3 Identify the most persuasive appeal. Will it be:
   - rational?
   - emotional?
   - fear?

4 Identify the most persuasive style. Will it be:
   - the product in use?
   - showing how the product will relate to and enhance the customers' lifestyle?
   - enacting customers' fantasy?
   - reflecting customers' mood?
   - using scientific/technical knowledge?
   - a testimonial?

5 Use the full potential of a headline. This is your chance to get the reader's attention. It should:
   - be very clear and state the unique selling proposition;
   - lead the reader to identify with the message;
   - be in the style of language the reader uses;
   - match the content of the rest of the advertisement;

6 Visual images used should:
   - reinforce the headline;
   - visualise the theme and the message;
   - have a main focal point;

7 Overall, does the copy:
   - grab attention?
   - relate positively to customers' beliefs and motivations?
   - identify a problem customers have and offer a solution?
   - generate interest via the item's appeal to customers?
   - reassure that needs will be satisfied?
   - promote action – inform the customers about availability?

■ The media

There are many means of communicating the message to your market segments, and the choice of media is as crucial as the message itself. Each medium of communication (for full guidance on using the Internet for advertising, see Chapter 9) from personal recommendation to television – has specific advantages

> *The choice of media is as crucial as the message itself.*

and limitations. Let's briefly consider some of the media available to a small business. As a rough rule of thumb, the more personal the advertising medium is, the more persuasive it is likely to be.

Personal recommendation by present customers to potential customers is perhaps the most persuasive means of attracting new custom. Obviously it is not one that can be used in the start-up period, but because of its power and zero cost it should be fostered with care as the business grows.

Direct 'personalised' calling by telephone or letter has the advantage of being able to target your communication precisely. It may have the effect of making a potential customer feel important and therefore more likely to respond in a positive manner. Others, however, may feel it an affront to their privacy. What would be the reaction of your target markets? Also, if the telephone is used, you have the opportunity to gain direct responses to your 'message'. Your approach, of course, must be carefully constructed and practised before use.

The average response rate from direct marketing is around 2 per cent. To improve on this figure, refer to the guidelines below.

Do-it-yourself direct marketing

- Clear market profiling is the key (see Chapter 3). Once profiles are compiled, communication media can be examined for match. If mailing lists are the preferred option, then these can be compiled in many ways:
  - from publicly available records such as the *Yellow Pages* and commercial telephone directories;
  - by contacting relevant associations and clubs, the members of which match your target profile (refer to association directories in your central reference library), as many associations and clubs, on application and payment of a fee, will provide a membership listing;
  - mailing lists to fit a wide variety of audience profiles are available from a range of mailing list brokers. A look through any issue of the magazine *Marketing* will reveal a number of companies advertising for busi-

ness. Mailing lists are also available from large organisations such as British Telecom.

- If buying in a mailing list, check:
  - what detail the listing gives – so you can see if it allows you to send the communication you want;
  - how up to date the listing is;
  - what the original purpose of the list was;
  - whether or not you will be able to sample the list; (communications are expensive so you don't want to find out the list mismatches after you have spent a couple of thousand pounds on a direct mailout);
  - what track record the listing has, what reliable evidence can be produced by the broker, what the success rate of previous mailings has been;
- The content and presentation of the message must be of a high quality, otherwise your communication will be seen as just another item of junk mail. All the guidelines that apply to message construction and presentation earlier in the chapter apply here, too. However, remember:
  - the singular aim of direct marketing is to get the required response;
  - the initial attention span of the recipient is likely to be low, so don't bore them to death – attention must be gained quickly and interest aroused if the rest of the communication is not to be skipped over and consigned to the waste paper bin;
  - lead with the appeal – the benefits to the purchaser or user – don't become bogged down in aimless preamble;
  - always think what impact the whole package will have on the recipient when it is first opened;
  - keep the direct mail you receive for the next month – review each piece with the aim of establishing examples of good practice and any styles to be avoided;
  - make sure the offer is clear and unambiguous;
  - make it easy for the audience to respond by including either a return envelope or link line telephone number (contact British Telecom for information on the 0800 service).
- Every response must be recorded. Ideally, you will use a computerised database system capable of producing personalised letters from cus-

tomer records. If you know little about computers, don't pay for expensive private training courses, sometimes costing in excess of £100 per day. Enquire at your local further dducation college. A small business micro, high-quality printer and database software can be obtained for less than £3000.

The *Yellow Pages* should be an obvious medium to use, particularly for specialist small businesses and SMEs. Many consumers use this as a starting point for finding goods and services. If you decide to pay for an entry, it is probably worth while to go for a distinctive box advertisement. Consumers are more likely to investigate the obvious rather than wade through the small print. Also, it is sensible if you can justify an entry under 'A' so that it is read first instead of last.

Newspaper advertising is very useful to a new business to build up awareness that it exists. The charge per advertisement can be quite high, but when compared to the potential number of readers it might be that the cost per customer reached can be low. However, the problem with newspapers, and the same is true of radio and TV, is that only a small percentage of the readership may be from the target market you are aiming at. If a large part of the local population is your target market, then this is certainly a good method to use. Remember to place advertisements where your potential customers will see them – the TV page, for instance, could be a good place to advertise video tapes.

A mention or feature in the local newspaper can sometimes be secured by new small businesses free of charge as a 'human interest' story. This is always worth investigating.

Magazines can be a useful medium to use where the readership corresponds to your target markets. Go to your local reference library and ask if they have a publication that details the characteristics of the readership of various magazines and find out if any match up with the profiles of your target markets. One advantage of using magazines over newspapers is that the magazine will be kept for quite a long period whereas the newspaper will be discarded after a day. The advertisement is therefore likely to be seen and read a greater number of times by each individual reader.

Local radio stations offer widespread coverage for a reasonable cost per thousand listeners. However, for effect, the advertisement would have to be repeated regularly over a period, considerably pushing up costs. If this medium is used, careful attention must be given to placing the advertisement at times when your target market is most likely to be listening.

Television is perhaps the most expensive form of advertising. However, short-duration 'spot' commercials are becoming reasonably priced. In the UK, Channel 4 provides considerable help for the first-time user.

Billboard posters are a relatively cheap form of communication. Usually you will have to pay a fee for the poster itself and then three months' rent of the billboard. If you decide to use this method, then the location must be chosen with care. Perhaps there is a large billboard close to where you plan to open your business, outside an office block where a large proportion of your target market works or on the bus route they use. Check out the site carefully: is it visible from more than just one direction, is there anything that will distract from whatever message it is attempting to send and will people have ample opportunity/time to see it?

The disadvantages of using posters are:

- research has been unable to gauge their effect (the general consensus is they are not very persuasive);
- people tend to regard them as part of the background, consequently the poster itself would have to be very creative to catch a person's attention.

Leaflets have the advantage over posters of being able to be targeted at specific groups of potential customers. They are relatively cheap to produce and circulate but are often ignored by the receivers – what did you do with the last lot of leaflets that were put through your letterbox? However, if you deliver to small areas at a time, it is relatively easy to monitor the results. Use the 'do-it-yourself direct marketing' guidelines to improve the effectiveness of leaflet design and distribution.

These are but a few of the main methods of communication. Here are some others for your consideration:

- diaries
- taxis
- exhibitions
- local charity magazines
- exterior of your business vehicles
- newsagents' windows
- beer mats
- milk bottles
- litter bins
- carrier bags
- interior and exterior of buses
- calendars
- sports team sponsorship
- packaging.

What others can you think of? The choice is certainly vast. Any single medium used on its own will be unlikely to be sufficient. Which do you select? To help you come to a decision, ask the following questions.

- Is it consistent with the image of your product?
- Will it be seen or heard in sufficient numbers by your target group?
- What opportunities will each target group have of seeing or hearing the advertisement?
- How many times will the target group see or hear the advertisement?
- What is the cost of reaching each individual customer?
- How persuasive do you consider the medium to be?
- Can it be targeted accurately for the group you wish to reach?
- Is it complementary to other media you plan to use?

■ How can the success of a sales promotion/advertisement be measured?

You should monitor the outcomes of your advertising and other sales promotion activities for two reasons:

- to compare the sales the campaign has generated against the costs involved to see whether or not it has been a profitable activity;
- to see whether or not the sales promotion has achieved its stated goals as then you can build on a good practice and make sure you don't make any mistakes twice.

There are several ways of doing this, but, as a general guide, you should plan and monitor your sales promotion campaigns as suggested in the forms shown in Figure 4.2.

■ Media audience profiles

Information on various media audience profiles is extensively researched and made available by a number of agencies:

- the Broadcasters' Advertising Research Board (BARB) provides information on television and radio;
- British Rate and Data (BRAD) lists virtually all types of advertising and their costs;
- the National Readership Survey (NRS) gives information on each publication's circulation and readership;
- Target Group Index, published by the British Market Research Bureau, available on a subscription basis, gives information that relates media to buying behaviour in specific markets.

MAKING THE SALE

The simple truth that nothing happens in business unless somebody makes a sale, emphasises the essential nature of the selling activity in the marketing mix.

Contrary to popular belief, selling skills can be learnt. It is certainly worth checking what courses are available in your locality. The alternative is to teach yourself. To this end, the following sections provide guidelines on the basic techniques of personal selling. I recommend that you study these and try to apply the techniques to your business, products and customers. As with any skill, practice will result in the development and sharpen-

> *Contrary to popular belief, selling skills can be learnt.*

Sales promotion plan

Objectives:

Duration (dates):

Theme or message:

Media to be used:

Cost:

In store promotional support (or personal contract support):

Implications for business organisation (e.g. capital and stock requirements):

Method to monitor and check results:

Measuring the success

Promotion:

Duration:

Theme/objective:

Media used: Comments

Total cost of campaign:

Estimated number exposed to campaign:

Of which estimated target marketing audience:

Sales objective:

Actual sales increase:

Variance (objective – results):

Increase in gross profits after cost of campaign:

(that is, actual sales increase x unit gross profit – total cost of campaign = £)

Fig. 4.2 Planning and monitoring your sales promotions

ing of your personal selling technique. You will obtain the best results by role-playing sales situations (perhaps with your husband, wife, partner, friend or colleague). You can learn a lot by doing this, particularly if you spend some time after each role-play trying to identify where you went wrong and what you did right. If you have the use of a video camera, a great deal can be learnt from taping and replaying each practice session.

A good salesperson is one who understands that the terms 'buying' and 'selling' describe different facets of the same business transaction, where the seller solves the buyer's problem and vice versa. Good selling practice focuses on and develops from identification of the buyer's problem. If you have successfully built the 'marketing approach' into your business operations, you should have the solutions to the customer's problem, and hence the sale, within your grasp. The rest is a matter of technique!

■ A framework for selling

Although there are no guaranteed success formulas, it is generally recognised that any sale moves through several logical steps as illustrated in Figure 4.3.

■ Pre-sale activity

The starting point must be identification of the target market (see Chapter 3). However, in the case of industrial and commercial selling, it is not enough to know which organisations to target. You need to select the right person in the organisation to present to. Generally, your aim is to get at the decision maker – the *Generally, your aim is to get at the decision maker – the person with the money, authority and need to buy.* person with the money, authority and need to buy (giving the rather sexist, but widely used, acronym MAN).

The next requirement is that you find out as much as you can about your customer's needs. You cannot offer the solution if you don't know the problem. With industrial and commercial customers, you will need to know and understand their business as well as they do.

Reading company reports, trade magazines and journals, making a positive attempt to understand the threats and opportunities your prospective client faces, and knowing your competition are all part of the professional salesperson's research objectives.

Out of financial necessity you must be selective. Personal selling is expensive, so you must endeavour to make it cost-effective by selecting the best prospects. 'Qualifying' prospective customers is a matter of shortlisting the ones that best match your capability to offer a solution to their 'problem' in a way that will result in a profit to you.

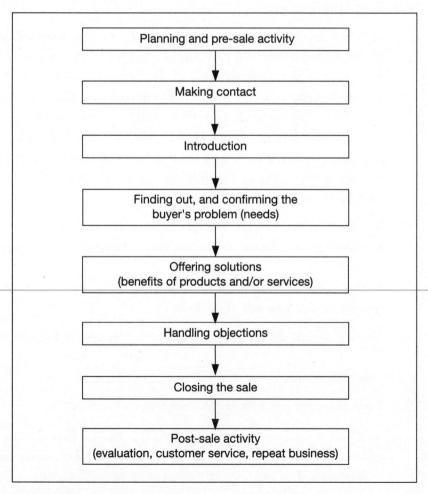

Fig. 4.3 The structure of a sale

Checklist

1 Can you identify whether or not they have a clear need for your product or service?

2 Have they the money and willingness to pay? What evidence is there that you can persuade them that paying for your 'solution' will represent 'value for money'?

3 Will they buy in large enough volume to make the sale viable?

4 Who will make the decision to purchase? Can you get to the one person who is the MAN. Or is the problem more complicated?

■ Getting appointments

Getting appointments is no easy matter. By far the best medium to use is the telephone. All calls should be kept short and you should stick to a well-rehearsed routine. The aim is to assess as many prospects as possible within a given period of time. Often a prospect will claim they are too busy to see you. The easiest way around this is to always offer an alternative time and date and then try to close the call that way. Never, ever try to overcome stronger objections; you are wasting time and money, move on to the next call. Follow a simple framework of:

■ courteous greeting and identification of the company;
■ move quickly on to relating a single benefit to the prospect's needs;
■ try to close the call by offering an alternative appointment date;
■ confirm the appointment details.

The whole call should not take more than a couple of minutes.

■ The sales interview

First, there are some basic rules to learn and remember.

■ Above all, be professional in both dress and manner. Be there on time and stick to whatever promises you made when arranging the interview. If you said you would only take 30 minutes of their time, don't take more.

- Don't waste time by talking about the weather or the decor of your prospect's office. Initial pleasantries are in order but should be brief. Remember that when you walk into the room you have an objective to meet. You have the initiative, so it is up to you to direct the interview. Don't lose the initiative in the first few minutes.

- Have a structure for your presentation, but, on the other hand don't stick religiously to some prepared script – otherwise you will come across as too smooth and slick and unbelievable – it will all appear as just so much 'salesman's talk'. Also avoid well-worn clichés, such as 'this is the best product on the market ... we have hundreds of satisfied customers'.

The structure of the interview can be built around the AIDA approach used to effect when discussing advertising and sales promotion. The first task is to get their attention, the second is to hold it by generating interest, the third to develop a desire to buy, so that you finally get the prospect to take the action of committing themselves to purchase (see Figure 4.4.).

You	The prospect
Lead with an initial benefit statement or open question.	Attention – listens and responds.
Ask 'open' questions – find out needs. Listen carefully. Ask closed questions – confirm needs.	Interest provides information.
	Desire – but may present objections.
Present the solution. State your product features and benefits – show how they will solve the problem.	
Resolve objections and attempt to close.	Action – order placed.

Fig. 4.4 The sales interview

You can open the sale by making an initial statement about the products you sell or, if you are uncertain about your prospect's needs, lead with an 'open' question. For example, a sales representative from a training organisation may open with: 'How could your staff training be improved?' Generally, open questions start with one of the following words:

'Who ...?' 'Why ...?' 'What ...?'
'When ...?' 'Where ...?' 'How ...?'

The open question encourages the prospect to talk about their business. It gets them involved and interested from the start. It is your opportunity to begin to establish the need.

Never lead with a closed question – you may not like the response. For example, 'Are you happy with the service your present suppliers give?' If the prospect replies 'yes' then you have perhaps just reached an embarrassing end to the interview! Closed questions have their place in confirming needs, controlling the interview and guiding the prospect along a pathway of reasoning that will result in a successful close. For example:

Salesperson: 'How could your staff training be improved?' (open question)
Prospect: 'The problem with using existing training courses at the local college, as we do at present, is that they are too general and the attendance times are often inconvenient.'
Salesperson: 'So, your company would benefit from a tailor-made package, shaped to your specific training needs?' (closed question – to confirm and underline first need/problem)
Prospect: 'Yes.'
Salesperson: 'And, it is also important that training takes place at a time and place that suits you?' (closed question – to confirm the second key need)
Prospect: 'Yes.'

In this simple example, the salesperson opened well. The first open question led to finding out two key needs. The following closed questions not only confirmed the problem but broke it down. Notice that the salesperson resisted combining the two closed questions into one. Double questions can not only confuse the prospect, they can make it look like you are 'lecturing to them'. Short and to the point closed questions are better. They keep the prospect involved in the interview and order their thoughts in the way you want them to 'travel'.

However, you must at all costs avoid turning the interview into an interrogation. Both the prospect and yourself must feel at ease. A prospect who does not 'open up' may be encouraged further without it seeming like an interrogation by using simple prompts such as:

'And?'
'Really?'
'Why is that?'
'Could you explain a little further?'

or simply by use of controlled silence to denote they should continue. These short open-ended questions will invariably get even the quiet or awkward prospects to open up.

Once you are sure you have isolated the prospect's needs, you can offer the solution. This should be done using the 'point out the features, sell the benefits' approach. This is where your (see Product and service decisions, at the beginning of this chapter) features–benefits analysis pays off.

■ Closing the sale

Many ask the question 'When should I start the attempt to close the sale?' The simple answer is that the close starts at the beginning of the sales interview. It is the logical result of a well-researched, planned and conducted interview.

The close starts at the beginning of the sales interview

The inexperienced approach the close with fear, apprehension and uncertainty. This is the bit they think will turn the prospect against them and sour the rapport they have built up through the interview. The problem is lack of confidence. If you have done your job properly, the prospect will want you to close, they will want their problem solved! Often the prospect will indicate that the time for your close is ripe by asking closed questions such as:

'What is the extent of your after-sales service?'

'What is the minimum order quantity?'

'How frequently can you deliver?'

'In what sizes and colours?'

'What discount do you offer on bulk purchases?'

Questions such as these tend to indicate they are more than interested, they want to buy. Don't miss the opportunity to close when it is handed to you. Have confidence, be enthusiastic.

In attempting to close, you will undoubtedly come across objections. Some will be genuine, some merely excuses for not buying and others the result of misunderstanding.

Genuine objections occur where there is a definite mismatch between what you are selling and what the prospect wants. If this is the case, then even though you will not make the sale, you can still gain a positive outcome by helping the prospect find the solution to their problem with another company. Even if this means giving a competitor business, the long-term benefit to you is the trust that ensues. The prospect may buy something else from you at another time. They are also likely to tell others about you. They may also recommend another company to you.

Misunderstandings are the easiest to rectify. However, if you come across many objections of this type it would seem to indicate that there is something wrong with your overall style and technique. Identify what is wrong and take action.

If you have correctly identified the prospect's problem and motivation, offered the right incentives to buy, communicated them well, then any objections the prospect puts in your path you can correctly identify as 'false' or 'excuses' for not buying. These can and should be overcome. False objections should never be addressed directly. They should be turned into reasons the prospect should buy. For example, counter price objections with value for money/benefit statements, such as, 'Even though our quote is higher than your present supplier, if you install our equipment what is your estimate of the savings you will make on wastage reduction in the first year?' Attempt to close after the prospect has responded with, 'Now, doesn't that mean doing business with us makes more sense in the longer term?'

Other objections relating to such factors as frequency of delivery, quality, reputation can be countered in similar ways. A small business may lack reputation, and be viewed as unreliable. The counter to this is that you can offer the prospect a quick and personal response to any problems. Refer them to testimonials from other customers.

Many prospects raise 'false objections' when they have to make a decision that will directly affect their success or failure within a company. You must reassure the prospect that they are making the right decision. The key is to identify and understand the prospect's personal motivations. It helps if you know who they are accountable to and for what.

SUMMARY

The marketing plan can only be put together after extensive research of:

- why your customers buy and who they are;
- the competition;
- the threats and opportunities posed by the wider business environment;
- your own strengths and weaknesses;

This information, researched and developed in this and the previous two chapters, allows you to develop a detailed marketing plan within the marketing mix framework of:

- product
- price
- place
- promotion.

Your decisions in each of these areas will add up to a unique selling proposition. This will represent what your business is and where it is going.

Advertising, sales promotion and personal selling are just the visible part of the marketing effort. Marketing starts with developing a product or service that the customer wants. In this way, the sales-person never ends up trying to sell a product nobody wants to buy.

Effective selling starts with the recognition that the salesperson's job is to solve the customer's problem. Selling is a skill that can be learnt. Marketing is something that pervades the whole business.

It is well worth remembering:

- the first point of contact with a customer – whether it be face to face, on the telephone or by letter – makes a lasting impression;
- where you are not selling a unique product (few businesses do), then it is the type or level of service provided that often clinches the sale;
- customers buy benefits not products;
- advertising, sales promotion and personal selling can be planned around the useful AIDA framework of attention, desire, interest and action.

Premises

1

2

3

4

5

6

7

8

9

10

INTRODUCTION

Unless you plan to run your business from home, you will need premises. Two of the key decisions that have to be made in acquiring premises are how big they should be and where they should be located. The size of your market and where it is located (see Chapter 3) and how it can be reached will have implications for your selection criteria for this asset.

CALCULATING SPACE REQUIREMENTS

You should take great care in calculating your space requirements for selling, storage and/or manufacture as once decided on and acquired they can prove difficult and costly to alter in the future. Careful thought should also be given to the future expansion rate. Will the selling/storage and/or manufacturing space be adequate to cope with your future plans?

The volume of physical sales will largely determine your space requirements. How much space you are liable to need for a given level of sales depends on what type of business you are in. Reference to government and trade statistics will often provide valuable indicators. For instance, statistics list the average

> *You should take great care in calculating your space requirements for selling, storage and/or manufacture.*

sales per given area for different types and sizes of retail operations. As you have an estimate of your turnover for your first year's trading, you can easily use this information to calculate your minimum space requirements (see Figure 5.1).

Other types of business may need more complicated approaches, involving the consideration of a number of variables. For instance, in a restaurant, the pressure exerted on selling space is a combination of projected number of meals to be sold and number of sittings possible in a given time period. This will, in turn, dictate the number of tables and chairs required and, hence, the selling space needed. If a restaurant needs to cater for 72 meals during its peak period from 8 pm to 10.30 pm and the average length of service time per table is 50 minutes, then the number of sittings possible will be

3 (that is, 150 minutes [length of peak period] /50 minutes [service time]). Therefore, the number of seats that will be required will be:

number of meals projected to be sold, 72/number of sittings, 3 = 24

Minimum selling space required	=	Projected sales per annum (derived from market research)
		Average sales per given area per annum for your type and scale of business (derived from government or trade-produced statistics)

Fig. 5.1 Using sales per given area statistics to estimate selling space requirements

If the owner intends to have four seats per table, then obviously six tables will be required. Assuming an allowance of 3.71 square metres for each table (including access), then the minimum space requirement for this restaurant will be 22.26 square metres (6 tables x 3.71 square metres [square metre requirement per table]).

Exercise

Identify what will determine your selling space requirements. Will it be one or a combination of the following:

- number of customers expected in a given period;
- the time it takes to complete an individual sale;
- the physical size of your products;
- special needs of customers (such as extra space requirements for the disabled, extra wide shopping aisles for people with prams and so on).

Calculate the minimum and maximum size of selling space you will need.

Manufacturing and administration space requirements will also be affected by volume of business. However, they will be modified by what plant and equipment you intend to acquire and what work organisation you have. What is important is that early on in the planning of your business, you should sketch out scale drawings of the optimum way of siting the necessary equipment.

Most businesses will need storage space for stock and raw materials. For those that trade in large volumes of physical stock, storage space will be directly determined by the stock levels maintained. In turn, the size of stock levels will be dictated by two factors: the sales level they will have to support and the frequency of deliveries they can secure.

FACTORS TO CONSIDER WHEN CHOOSING A LOCATION

There may be a number of premises of the right size to choose from, but will they be in the right place? Usually the characteristics of your target markets – normally their various locations – will provide the key to deciding where to locate your premises. However, there are other considerations that should be weighed in the balance. For instance, the nature of your product or service might require the close proximity and availability of skilled labour, back-up services, stock and raw materials sup-

Usually the characteristics of your target markets – normally their various locations – will provide the key to deciding where to locate your premises.

pliers. The scale of the finance available to you may preclude city centre and main road locations. Your goal of a rapid growth rate might make some areas of good but relatively static growth undesirable.

Exercise

Think very carefully about what your business will need in terms of location. Draw up a list of locational criteria by assessing the applicability and importance of the following factors to your business.

Geographical concentrations of your market(s)
The pertinent question here is, will your customers come to you or will you go to them? If your customers are going to come to you, then obviously you will need to be located as close to them as possible. If you will be going to your customers, then your premises will have to be located where there is easy access to efficient road, rail and air networks for sale and distribution of your goods/services.

The needs and buying behaviour of your customers
In the course of your market research, you should have identified the needs of your customers and translated them into the benefits your busi-

ness should provide to fulfil those needs. What locational attributes should your business premises have to cater for your customers' needs and buying behaviour? For example, convenience might dictate that your premises should be close to a system of transport your customers use (such as bus routes and bus stops, car parking facilities and so on). In some product and service markets, customers habitually shop around before making a buying decision – good examples of this being female fashion and estate agents. Therefore, if your markets display similar buying behaviour, you should find premises that are in the same area as your competition. In this way the cluster of similar businesses can act as a magnet, drawing customers in.

The image of your product/service
The area in which you locate must be consistent with the overall image of your business. A retailer of designer clothes would probably lack credibility trading in a run-down inner city area.

Evidence of market decline in a locality
A number of vacant premises or businesses for sale in the area should raise serious doubts about the potential of such a location. What has gone wrong? Find out.

Future changes to a location that might affect trade
The ideally located premises that you have found might not be as attractive in the future when the bus route is moved, parking restrictions are imposed in front of your premises and the new road cuts off your passing trade.

BUY OR LEASE?

There is no 'right answer' to this one, it is a matter for you to decide in relation to your business' requirements. Here are some of the factors to consider.

Buying a freehold property is a major capital investment. The main disadvantage is obvious: you will have to find the finance (see Chapter 8) for the purchase. The repayments and cost of that finance will probably prove to be more than outgoings associated with a leasehold purchase. However, you will be buying an asset that will appreciate in value and, thus, in future years, it should provide a sound base for raising further finance for expansion. With the purchase of a lease, the opposite is true – as the years on the lease are used up, it will depreciate in value. Further, because of the lack of permanence with a lease and the fact that it decreases in value, you will find it more difficult to raise finance for its

> *There are more constraints and controls attached to the operation of a business from a leasehold than freehold premises.*

acquisition. The opposite is true for freehold property – you will find a range of financial institutions prepared to make long-term loans on such an investment.

Generally, you will find that there are more constraints and controls attached to the operation of a business from a leasehold than freehold premises. Both will, of course, be subject to planning permission, but the leasehold agreement is more than likely to contain clauses imposing repair and maintenance obligations, and restrictions on uses and alterations.

PLANNING PERMISSION AND LICENCES

The golden rule here is to double-check that the premises you intend to acquire can, in fact, be used for all the activities you intend to carry out now and, just as important, in the future. This is just as true with the purchase of an existing business.

The main categories of use are:

- retail
- office
- light industrial
- general industrial

Within each broad category, there are further subdivisions. In the first instance, check with your local authority planning office and later in detail with your solicitor. You should also note that you will need planning permission for any alterations, including new shop fronts and signs. Further, most alterations and extensions will have to conform to building regulations. The main thing to note here is that seeking such permission can be a lengthy and sometimes costly process. You will certainly need legal advice and, more than likely, the services of an architect and surveyor.

You must also check with your local authority as to whether or not the existence of any local by-laws will impose any restrictions or controls on your business. A licence, registration or other permissions may also be needed (see Chapter 9).

 Summary and checklist

For many, particularly retail businesses, acquisition of the right premises is perhaps one of the most important decisions ever made in a business career. Use the following checklist to help you make sure you have got it right.

1 Have you calculated your present and future space requirements?

2 Which of the following are important factors in determining best location (rank them in order to use as a check list):
 - closeness to customers' homes, places of work and so on;
 - parking facilities;
 - transport facilities for customers;
 - proximity to competitors (that is, your customers like to shop around);
 - proximity to other customer magnets (such as, banks, large stores, bus stops, sunny side of the street, main shopping areas and so on);
 - cheap and efficient access to suppliers;
 - proximity to labour force;
 - image of area;
 - other ...?

3 Have you severe restrictions on the amount you can borrow?

4 If so, have you considered a lease instead of freehold?

5 Alternatively, a different form of distribution (see Chapter 4)?

6 If buying a lease, have you:
 - obtained legal advice?
 - checked that the present owner has the right to sell the lease?
 - checked all the details of the lease?
 - the rent might be acceptable now, but a fundamental aspect of leases are rent reviews – have you discussed this with your solicitor?
 - checked the attitude of financial institutions to your borrowing requirements for such a lease?
 - other ...?

7 Have you obtained planning permission?

8 Have you taken into account any future uses your business may put the property to as it expands?

9 If buying freehold, are there any covenants in the deeds that will pose a threat to your business?

10 How easily will you be able to find a buyer for the premises if the business fails?

11 Have you checked whether or not any local by-laws apply?

12 Have you calculated the full cost of the premises:
- legal fees for buying, planning permission, licence applications and so on;
- surveying fees;
- cost of finance;
- advance rent;
- rates;
- alterations and improvements;
- costs of conforming with environmental health and health and safety regulations;
- insurances;
- service connection charges;
- if you are already in business, costs to disturbance of business (loss of sales and so on);
- other ...?

Will you make a profit

INTRODUCTION

The previous chapter should have helped you establish the scale of demand for your product or service and a range of prices potential customers might be prepared to pay. The next step is to establish whether or not the costs involved in exploiting the market will result in a large enough profit to warrant investigating the business idea further.

The solution to the problem is, at first sight, simple. Reasonably, you may think it is a matter of establishing the revenue you will earn from your market and deducting all the costs in selling and/or producing your product/service.

To see whether or not this is true, let's take an imaginary example of a business making and selling widgets. To keep the example simple, the business has two costs: rent and equipment costs per annum of £10,000 and a raw material cost of £1.00 per widget. The business has estimated it will sell 20,000 widgets in its first year's trading. With a prevailing market price of £2.00, it sets out to estimate its profit.

Sales volume revenue (20,000 × £2.00)		£40,000
Rent and equipment costs	£10,000	
Raw materials costs (20,000 × £1.00)	£20,000	
Total costs		£30,000
Profit		£10,000

The business will be profitable or will it? What will happen if the sales drop by half? Will this result in the profits being halved to £5000? The answer is no, because not all of the costs have the same characteristics. Logically, the raw materials cost will be reduced by half in proportion with the drop in sales – not as many raw materials need to be purchased. But what about the other costs? The business will still have to pay rent on the premises and maintain its equipment regardless of how many it sells – these costs will remain the same. The business will not be profitable.

Sales revenue (10,000 × £2.00)		£20,000
Rent and equipment costs	£10,000	
Raw materials costs (10,000 × £1.00)	£10,000	
Total costs		£20,000
Profit		Zero!

You should be able to see that for this business to operate at a profit, it would have to do one or a combination of the following:

- increase its sales volume;
- increase the selling price;
- reduce its costs.

However, attempts to change one factor to the advantage of the business may inadvertently bring about a disastrous change in another. For example, if the selling price of widgets is increased to £2.50 in an attempt to offset the effect of the fall in sales, customers may go elsewhere to seek cheaper prices, possibly cutting the already reduced sales volume by half. This would put the business in an even worse position.

Sales revenue (5000 × £2.50)		£12,500
Rent and equipment costs	£10,000	
Raw materials costs (5000 × £1.00)	£5,000	
Total costs		£15,000
Loss		£2,500

This very simple example clearly shows that the task of estimating profit is not as simple as it first appears. The factors that determine profit – costs, sales volume and selling price – are all intertwined. Altering one factor can have a marked effect on one or all of the others.

The task of estimating profit is not as simple as it first appears.

To be able to predict the profit or loss your business venture could make, what is needed is some method or model capable of clearly calculating and showing the impact of changes in any one of these factors on the profitability of your intended business. A model that will answer all those 'if …, what? questions, such as 'If I fail to meet my sales target by 10 per cent, what will my total profits be?' or 'If my stock costs rise by 15 per cent how many more do I need to sell to maintain my profits?' and so on. To build up this model, all of its components – cost, selling price, sales volume – have to be examined in much more detail.

YOUR COSTS

■ Not all expenditure is a cost!

Before proceeding to examine the characteristics and structure of costs in detail, it is important for you to understand what is and what isn't a cost to a business. Otherwise you may fall into the trap of classifying all the expenditure you make in relation to your business as a cost.

> *It is important for you to understand what is and what isn't a cost to a business.*

Money going into a business is soaked up into two distinct areas: the costs the business incurs and its capital requirements (for a full discussion of the characteristics of capital, see Chapter 7). To be able to easily distinguish between expenditure on costs and capital, you would be well advised to remember the following working definitions.

- **Cost** is the value of something the business has used.
- **Capital** is the value of something the business has.

To illustrate, if a business buys in £20,000-worth of stock at the beginning of the month and has £5000-worth left at the end of the month, then £15,000 of stock will have been sold (discounting the possibility of theft and wastage). This, having been used up in the business, will be a cost, while the £5000 of stock left on the shelves, being something the business has, will be capital.

Exercise

Try to determine which items from the following list of expenditure made by a taxi proprietor in his first year represent capital investment in the business and which are definitely costs:

	£
Car	5,500
Fare meter	500
Expenditure on maintenance	1,000
Petrol and oil	3,000

You would be right to identify the expenditure on maintenance charges, petrol and the oil as costs, as those items will have been used up by the business in the course of the year. On the other hand, you cannot count all of the expenditure on the car and the fare meter as a cost because the taxi proprietor will still possess both items at the end of the year. However, it is obvious that the car and the meter, by being used in the business, will have lost value – they will have depreciated. The amount by which they have depreciated can be counted as a cost.

The important thing to remember is that the cost of major capital purchases (known as fixed assets) are spread out over their working life. For example, a van costing £8000 with an expected working life of four years could be depreciated at £2000 per annum.

When finance has been secured to acquire major items, newcomers to business often make the mistake of double-counting the cost by counting both loan repayments and the depreciation as costs to the business. The loan repayment is not a cost to the business – it is simply a repayment of capital and, as such, it must come out of profits. However, any fees connected with arranging the finance and interest payable are costs.

To determine what depreciation costs your business will incur, you will need to identify what your major purchases will be (see Chapter 7) and then adopt a suitable method of providing for depreciation. You may care to use the next section to select a method or decide to leave it to your accountant.

■ Methods of providing for depreciation

There are several ways of providing for depreciation of assets. Here I briefly consider three of the most popular.

- straight line method;
- the production hour method;
- reducing balance method.

All of the following methods allocate the same total amount for depreciation – that is, the full cost of the purchase less resale value (if any). It is the timing of the costs that differentiates each method.

The straight line method seeks to spread the cost of the asset evenly over its working life. As it is simple to work out, it is commonly used, but only really suitable for assets whose resale value of which declines with time and not usage. The calculation for determining annual depreciation is:

$$\frac{\text{Original cost (or revaluation)} - \text{Resale value}}{\text{Working life (years)}}$$

For example, if a cold store cabinet is bought for £4000 with a planned life with the business of 4 years and an estimated resale value of £2000, then the annual rate of depreciation will be £500.

The production hour method is more suitable for assets such as machinery, the resale value of which may be largely determined by how many hours (or miles and so on) they have been worked. The calculation again is simple:

$$\frac{\text{Depreciation}}{\text{per hour}} = \frac{\text{Original cost (or revaluation)} - \text{Resale value}}{\begin{array}{c}\text{Working life in units of usage}\\\text{(such as hours, miles and so on)}\end{array}}$$

For example, if a machine is bought for £20,000 with a planned working life of 80,000 hours, then the hourly depreciation would be £0.25. If the machine is operated for 160 hours in one month, then the monthly depreciation cost will be £40.00.

Both of the above methods fail to take into account the commonly known fact that many assets can lose a higher proportion of their second-hand value in their early life. You will have no doubt recognised this in the many domestic purchases you have made – cars, TVs, washing machines and so on. The reducing balance method seeks to take this into account by attributing larger depreciation costs in the earlier years. This is done by decreasing the value of the asset by a fixed percentage each year. The result is to allocate costs on a 'diminishing sliding scale' as time goes by. However, using this method, the value of an asset is never reduced to zero!

The formula for calculating the percentage rate to be used is:

$$\frac{\text{Annual percentage}}{\text{Rate of depreciation}} = 1 - n\sqrt{\frac{\text{Residual value}}{\text{Cost}}} \times 100$$

Note: n is the useful life of the asset.

This calculation looks difficult, but is relatively simple with a modern calculator that has logarithm capability. You don't have to understand why the calculation works, only how to operate it. On most calculators, the procedure is as laid out in Figure 6.1. If you have got such a calculator, try to apply the reducing balance method on the information in the cold store cabinet example – you will find the solution and the comparison of the methods in Figure 6.2.

1. Enter the residual value	2. Press divide
3. Enter the original cost or revaluation	4. Press the equals key
5. Press the log key	6. Press divide
7. Enter the useful life of asset	8. Press the equals key
9. Press inv (invert) and then the log key (to obtain the anti log)	10. Press multiply
11. Enter 100 and press equals	12. Finally, subtract the answer from 100

Fig. 6.1 Using a calculator to obtain the annual percentage rate of depreciation (reducing balance)

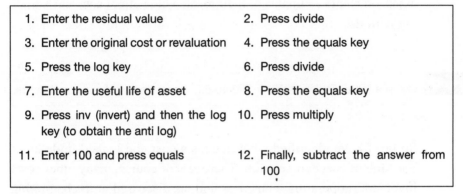

$$\text{Annual percentage rate of depreciation} = 1 - \sqrt[4]{\frac{£2000}{£4000}} \times 100$$

$$= 15.9\%$$

Yr end	Reducing balance method			Straight line method		
	Net value	Depreciation		Net value	Depreciation	
		Annual	Cumulative		Annual	Cumulative
Start	4000	–	–	4000	–	–
1	3364	636	636	3500	500	500
2	2829	535	1171	3000	500	1000
3	2379	450	1621	2500	500	1500
4	2000	379	2000	2000	500	2000

Fig. 6.2 The reducing balance and straight line methods compared

The reducing balance method may be more complicated to calculate, but, for many assets, it will better reflect reality. It evens out the asset's operating costs over time by counterbalancing the decline in depreciation by the increasing maintenance costs as the asset becomes worn with usage.

In selecting your method, you must give careful consideration to the type of asset and how it will lose value. In the end, you may wish to ignore the above methods and calculate the depreciation of your assets on sound estimates of their resale value after each year's trading periods.

Exercise

Using a table similar to that in Figure 6.3, estimate your fixed asset costs.

So far, I have identified what defines a cost and looked in detail at one kind of cost depreciation. There are, of course, many other costs involved in operating a business and, as discussed at the beginning of the chapter, certain costs afe affected in different ways to changes in sales volume. We must now turn our attention to classifying the costs involved in running your business.

Item	Total cost (£)	Life years	Depreciation first year (£)	Comments
1. 2. 3. 4. 5.				
Total capital		Total first year		

Fig. 6.3 Charting the cost of your fixed assets

■ Fixed costs

These are the costs you will have to pay whether your business is doing well or badly. A good test to apply to determine whether or not an item is a fixed cost is to ask the question, 'If I don't sell anything at all will I still have to pay out for this item?' If you will, then it is definitely a fixed cost. For example, a shop will still have items such as rent, electricity and permanent pay even if no customers come into the shop. Over short periods of time – say less than a year – these costs will change very little no matter how much you sell – they are 'fixed' and not affected by changes in sales volume. Obviously, over a longer period they may change as you take on more staff, buy extra machinery or move to larger premises.

It is possible now to start to build a model of how costs, sales volume, selling price and profit interact together by drawing up a simple chart to show how fixed costs behave in relation to sales volume (see Figure 6.4).

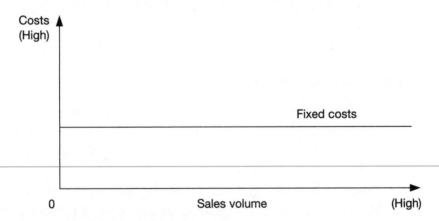

Fig. 6.4 Sales volume and fixed costs

■ Variable costs

These are costs that do vary when there are changes in sales volume – hence the term 'variable'. Their key characteristic is that they will rise or fall in direct proportion with rises or falls in sales volume. For most businesses, the main variable cost will be raw materials and

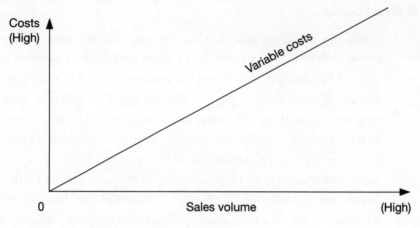

Fig. 6.5 Sales volume and variable costs

other stocks. It is easy to see that these will vary in direct proportion with how much is sold or manufactured.

The model can now be taken one step further by drawing a graph of how variable costs change according to sales volume changes (see Figure 6.5).

■ Costs and sales volume

Now both types of cost can be brought together and it can be seen how the unit cost (that is, the cost of selling/producing each product) is affected by sales volume. Let's take a simple example to illustrate the effect.

Hifas is a small business producing and selling knitwear. Its fixed costs for one year of trading are estimated at £10,000 and the cost of materials to make 1 jumper (its unit variable cost) is £2.00. Hifas' total variable costs will, of course, vary for different levels of sales. Thus, 15,000 sales will result in £30,000 variable costs; 5000 sales will cost £10,000, and so on. Figure 6.6 shows the relationship between its fixed and variable costs over a range of sales levels.

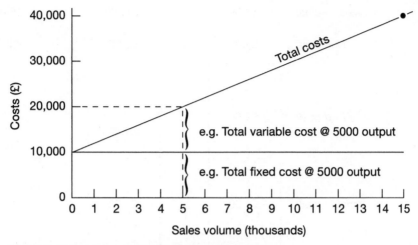

Fig. 6.6 Sales volume, fixed and variable costs

The total cost of producing each sale can easily be calculated from Figure 6.6 by dividing total costs for a given level of sales by the number sold. Let's have a look at the total unit cost for a range of sales volumes.

Sales	Total cost	Unit cost
	£	£
5,000	20,000	4.00
10,000	30,000	3.00
15,000	40,000	2.66

You can see that for higher sales levels, the cost of producing and selling each item is reduced. The variable cost per unit will remain the same, but the fixed costs per unit are reduced as they are spread out over a greater output (that is, total fixed costs divided by output = unit fixed costs):

The cost of each unit of sale obviously sets a bottom line on the price you can charge and still make a profit. If the highest price Hifas could set is £3.00, then, it would certainly make a profit with 15,000 sales per annum, but quite a large loss if there were only 5000 sales. At a sales level of 10,000 units it would make neither a loss nor a profit – this is known as its breakeven point. It is critical for any business to know where this point is, when sales revenue will begin to overtake costs and produce a profit.

Sales volume:	5,000	10,000	15,000
Unit cost:	£4.00	£3.00	£2.66

Fixed cost:	£2.00	£1.00	£0.66
Variable cost:	£2.00	£2.00	£2.00

THE BREAKEVEN POINT:

SALES VOLUME, COSTS, SELLING PRICE AND PROFIT

Selling price can now be added to the model to complete the picture of how the sales volume, cost and selling price interact to produce a profit or loss.

Let's continue with the knitwear example and add the sales revenue line to the graph of sales volume and costs. To do this, first a possible selling price has to be selected say, £4.00 – which is thenmultiplied by a selected output – say, 10,000 units (to give a sales revenue for that level of sales, £40,000), and this point is marked on the graph.

> *The point where the sales revenue line intersects the total costs line is where the business will be making just sufficient revenue to cover all costs. This is the breakeven point (BEP).*

Second as the sales revenue will rise and fall in direct proportion with rises and falls in sales, all you need to do is take a ruler and draw a line from the point of zero revenue) through the point just marked on the graph. The result is shown in Figure 6.7.

The point where the sales revenue line intersects the total costs line is where the business will be making just sufficient revenue to cover all costs. This is the breakeven point (BEP). Below that sales volume, the business will make a loss; above, it will make a profit. Drawing the graph helps you to quickly see and read off the various profits or losses you could make for any given level of sales.

Try it for yourself. Take a sheet of graph paper and redraw Figure 6.7. What profit or loss will Hifas make at the following sales volumes: 3000, 7000, 12,000, 14,000?

You can turn the graph into a more dynamic model by adding different sales revenue lines to gauge the effect of different selling prices.

What will the breakeven points be for selling prices of £3.50, £3.00 and £2.50? In other words, how much more in each case would Hifas have to sell to reach breakeven on these reduced selling prices? Add the new revenue lines to your graph to find out.

■ Gross profit and breakeven

As has just been seen, you can work out the BEP by drawing a graph. You can also use a formula to achieve the same ends:

$$BEP = \frac{Fixed}{Unit\ selling\ price - Unit\ variable\ cost}$$

Unit selling price minus unit variable cost gives the gross profit per unit of sale. For example, if you are selling records, the difference between what you pay for one (its cost price) and what you sell it at (selling price) is the amount you have left over to pay fixed costs, and hopefully, retain some net profit for yourself (see Figure 6.8). As the gross profit on each item of sale has to contribute to the payment of the fixed costs, you will have to make enough individual gross profits (contributions) to cover fixed costs to reach breakeven. The above formula can thus be simplified to:

127

$$BEP = \frac{\text{Gross profit}}{\text{Fixed costs}}$$

Let's substitute some figures from our example to demonstrate. With a selling price of £4.00 and variable costs of £2.00, Hifas makes a gross profit of £2.00 per unit of sale. As its fixed costs are £10,000, it will have to sell 5000 items to cover its fixed costs and reach breakeven (5000 × £2.00 unit gross profit = £10,000).

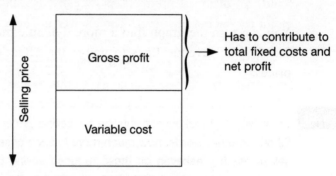

Fig. 6.8 The structure of a cost

Exercise To gain some experience in using the formula, check the answers that you obtained from the graph with the formula.

■ Multiproduct breakeven points

You can now see the finished model, which was started at the beginning of the chapter, but the probability is that it will not fit the requirements of your intended business. The model only deals with a business selling one kind of product, which is very rare. Thus, in this section, two methods for calculating the breakeven sales point for businesses selling a range of different products will be considered.

The first method offers a simple solution where the percentage profit margin can be derived from published statistics. The second method is more complicated, but provides more information in giving breakeven sales figures for individual products or product groups by allocating fixed costs on the proportion of total gross profits each product is expected to earn. Both methods are explained with the use of comprehensive examples. You would be well advised to have a calculator on hand to enable you to follow them through and thereby improve your understanding.

■ Using the gross profit percentage margin

If you are running a shop, you could be selling hundreds, if not thousands, of different products. How can you calculate the breakeven point for such a business? The answer is perhaps simpler than you might think.

Retail businesses common to a particular type, such as newsagents and small grocery shops, tend to operate to a set gross profit margin. This is because they tend to sell in similar markets and buy in stock at similar cost prices. The gross profit margin – which is simply the gross profit expressed as a percentage of the sales – can thus be substituted in the BEP formula for actual gross profit:

$$BEP = \frac{\text{Fixed cost}}{\% \text{ gross margin}}$$

For example, a small grocery shop with an expected margin of 20 per cent and fixed costs of £10,000 per annum would calculate its breakeven point as follows:

$$BEP = \frac{£10,000}{20\% \text{ (i.e. } 20/100)}$$

$$BEP = \frac{£10,000}{0.2}$$

$$BEP = £50,000$$

This, too, can be shown in graph form. The graph is constructed as before, but this time the variable costs and revenue line is omitted and replaced by a gross profit line. Figure 6.9 illustrates the breakeven point for the small grocery shop.

The gross profit line is drawn by first selecting a sales volume –

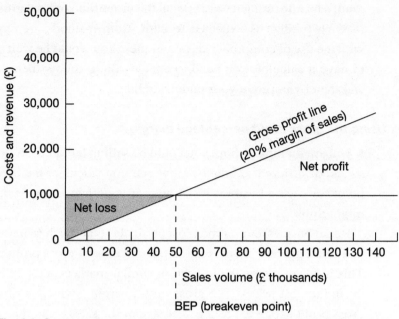

Fig. 6.9 Constructing a breakeven chart using a gross profit margin

£100,000 in the example – then calculating how much gross profit the volume of sales will produce with a given margin (20 per cent in the example) – in this case, it will be 20 per cent of £100,000, which is £20,000 gross profit – and marking the profit against the level of sales on the graph. The gross profit line is then drawn with a ruler from zero gross profit/zero sales (obviously, zero sales will result in zero profit) through the marked point on the graph. You can see that the graph gives the same sales, £50,000, to reach breakeven as the formula method does.

Exercise

Try constructing your own graph. The business may not be able to achieve the breakeven sales figure. What sales figure would it have to achieve to reach breakeven if it charged slightly higher prices and operated on a 25 per cent margin?

To give you some more practice, let's presume the business faces higher stock costs and therefore has to operate on a reduced margin of 15 per cent. With a 15 per cent margin, what is the new BEP? What sales level will have to be achieved to make a net profit of £10,000?

You can either construct a graph and plot all of the different gross profit lines (that is 15, 20 and 25 per cent) or use the formula. Work with the method you find the easiest.

....

■ Allocating fixed costs to each product on the basis of gross profit earned

If you intend to sell/produce a range of products, all with different profit margins and no published or accepted percentage margin to use as a guide, you can still use the breakeven formula. You have to decide on some method of apportioning the fixed costs to each product or product group. There are several ways of doing this.

One, not unreasonable, method is to allocate fixed costs to each product on the basis of the percentage of total gross profits each is expected to generate. Simply, a product that generates more gross profit than another will be called on to 'pay' a larger share of the overheads. However, do not mistake a large profit margin on a product as an indicator that it will produce the largest gross profit. It is the number of times that profit margin is earned (sales × profit margin) that is important. Clearly it is better to sell 10,000 items at a penny profit per item than 10 items at £1 profit per item!

Although in the planning stage you cannot forecast the sales of each product precisely, you can estimate the percentage of total sales of each product precisely. In other words, your market research should be able to tell you which product you are likely to sell the most of and which the least. As you can also estimate your variable costs and the selling prices, you can also calculate your gross profit margin on each product. Having collected this information you are now in a position to allocate overheads on the basis of the proportion of total profits each product is expected to produce. For example, if you intend to sell two products, which we shall call A and B, with respective profit margins of 30 and 40 per cent, and product A is expected to sell 3 times as much as product B, so that A will generate 75 per cent of the sales and B 25 per cent, then fixed costs would be allocated to each product by calculating the ratio (proportion) of A to B in providing total gross profit, as follows:

	Sales	×	Margin	= Gross profit
A:	75	×	30	= 2250
B:	25	×	40	= 1000

This gives a ratio of 2250:1000, simplified by cancelling down to 9:4. Therefore, fixed costs will be apportioned:

$$9/13 \times 100 = 69.23\% \text{ to product A}$$
$$4/13 \times 100 = 30.77\% \text{ to product B}$$

With overheads of £1000, £692 will be allocated to A and £308 to B. The breakeven point can then be calculated using the standard formula BEP = Fixed costs/Gross margin, which would be £2306 for product A and £770 for product B. This gives a total breakeven sales figure for the business of £3076. The same result can be achieved by modifying the standard breakeven formula to include the above information:

$$\text{BEP} = \cfrac{\text{Fixed costs}}{\underset{(\%S \times P) \quad + \quad (\%S \times P)}{\text{Product A} \qquad\qquad \text{Product B}}}$$

$$\text{BEP} = \frac{£1000}{(0.75 \times 0.30) \; + \; (0.25 \times 0.4)}$$

$$\text{BEP} = \frac{£1000}{0.225 + 0.1}$$

$$\text{BEP} = \frac{£1000}{0.325}$$

$$\text{BEP} = £3076$$

Let's take a more realistic example to explore the process in more detail. Eastern Fried (an imaginary business), a fast food outlet, plans to sell three products: chicken burger, standard chicken and family bucket. Management has researched the market and costs, and the selling prices and variable costs are as follows:

	Chicken burger	Standard chicken	Family bucket
Selling price	1.00	2.00	4.00
Variable cost	0.50	1.50	2.40
Gross profit (contribution)	0.50	0.50	1.60
Percentage margin (profit/selling price × 100)	50%	25%	40%

Eastern Fried don't expect to sell the products in equal amounts. Market research estimates that the business' total £ sales for the coming year will be made up as follows:

- 30 per cent of £ sales will be chicken burgers;
- 50 per cent of £ sales will be standard chickens;
- 20 per cent of £ sales will be family buckets.

Eastern Fried's fixed costs are estimated at £10,000 per annum.

To calculate the total sales needed to reach breakeven, Eastern Fried use an extended version of the breakeven formula:

$$BEP = \frac{\text{Fixed costs}}{\underset{(\%S \times P)}{\text{Product X}} + \underset{(\%S \times P)}{\text{Product Y}} + \underset{(\%S \times P)}{\text{Product Z}}}$$

Notes:

X = chicken burgers
Y = standard chickens
Z = family buckets
%S = percentage of total sales in each product
P = gross profit (contribution) produced by the product

- If the sales percentage represents physical units of sale, then the gross profit must be expressed in money. Accordingly, the breakeven sales figure will be in physical units.
- If the sales percentage represents £ sales, then the gross profit figure must be expressed as a percentage margin. Accordingly, the breakeven sales figure will be in pounds.

133

Using the formula we can obtain the total sales in pounds Eastern Fried needs to reach breakeven:

$$BEP = \frac{£10,000}{(0.3 \times 0.5) + (0.5 \times 0.25) + (0.2 \times 0.4)}$$

$$= \frac{£10,000}{0.355}$$

$$= £28,169$$

As the percentages of total sales of each product are known, it is easy to calculate the breakeven sales (£) for each product. In addition, to prove the 'external formula' works, let's calculate the gross profit each product will contribute to fixed costs to see whether or not it is sufficient:

Product	% of total sales	Breakeven sales (£)	Margin (%)	Gross profit
Burgers	30	8,451	50	4,226
Chickens	50	14,085	25	3 521
Buckets	20	5,633	40	2,253
	100%	£28,169		£10,000

To calculate the number that has to be sold is a simple matter of dividing sales by selling price for each product. In this case, Eastern Fried would have to sell 8451 chicken burgers, 7042 standard chickens and 1408 family buckets in the coming year just to reach breakeven. This works out at 162 burgers, 135 standard chickens and 27 family buckets per week.

The calculations involved to achieve the breakeven figure for this example seem tedious, but, with practice, they can be done quite quickly. If you build this multiproduct breakeven model using a computer spreadsheet, you can substitute a range of selling prices and costs and recalculate the BEP with ease – this will greatly help decisions relating to prices, costs and sales mix.

When this calculation has been done once, you can easily obtain an overall percentage gross profit margin for the sales mix and transfer the information to a graph to study the effect on profits over a range of sales volumes. Eastern Fried's expected gross margin from its sales mix is easily calculated by dividing BEP gross profit by BEP total sales and multiplying the result by 100 – that is £10,000/£28,169 × 100 = 35.5 per cent gross profit margin on sales.

■ The breakeven profit point (BEPP)

We have already used the model to identify the profits that will be earned with varying combinations of sales volumes, costs and selling prices. However, it would be advantageous to start with a desired profit and proceed directly to calculate the level of sales required to achieve it. Calculation of the breakeven profit point is simply a matter of adding your profit goal to fixed costs and dividing the result by the gross profit/contribution per unit of sale:

$$\text{BEPP} = \frac{\text{Fixed costs} + \text{Desired profits}}{\text{Unit gross profit}}$$

In other words, you are asking the question, 'How many individual contributions of gross profit will have to be made to cover both fixed costs and my desired profit?'

Suppose, in the above example, the owners of Eastern Fried had to meet a profit goal of £15,000, then the breakeven profit point would be:

$$\text{BEPP} = \frac{£10\,000 + £15\,000}{35.5\% \ (\text{i.e. } 35.5/100 = 0.355)}$$

$$\text{BEPP} = \frac{£25,000}{0.355}$$

$$\text{BEPP} = £70,423$$

As the percentages of total sales of each product, you may like to work out BEPP for each product.

■ Estimating your target profit

As has been seen, if your estimates and classification of costs is accurate, you can use the breakeven model to readily identify the sales volume necessary to generate a desired net profit. The unanswered question is, 'What target profits should you be aiming for?' The answer 'To make a living' is not enough, nor is some figure off the top of your head. Out of net profits, you will have to provide for the following.

- What you consider to be sufficient living expenses for yourself. You may use your present pay plus an allowance for inflation, but you must add on the non-pay benefits associated with employment, such as sick pay and pension schemes, that you will only receive at additional cost when you become self-employed.
- Repayment of capital loans less interest.
- Allowance for retaining some profits in the business to finance future capital requirements (see Chapter 7). Although the replacement of fixed assets is partly allowed for in the cost of depreciation, you would be well advised to remember that the replacement cost may be well in excess of the original purchase price. Thus, you will have to find the difference out of profits or take on another capital loan. Many businesses face bankruptcy after their first few years because they have failed to allow for sufficient profits to be retained to finance further expansion.

Further, you should be seeking a profit that represents a satisfactory return on the money invested in the business. The profits earned by your business should be greater than the return you would get if the money (yours or borrowed) was invested elsewhere, say a savings account. For example, with an interest rate of 10 per cent, say, offered on savings accounts, £100,000 invested in a business should produce net profits well in excess of £10,000 per annum, otherwise the owner might as well stay in bed and put the money in the bank. Further, while there is virtually no risk of not getting your money plus interest back from a savings account, an investment in a small business is fraught with risk. You should be aiming for profits that will represent a far higher return on capital invested than could be offered by a savings account. The riskier your business, the higher the rate of return on capital invested should be.

Calculate what your minimum profits per annum should be to represent a satisfactory return on your investment by:

- finding out the current rate of interest (before tax) on savings accounts;
- adding on a percentage for the element of risk involved – for an entirely new product this will be high (say 30 per cent), for a tried and tested business this will be low (say 10 per cent);
- calculating the average capital that will be employed in the business over its trading year (see Chapter 7);
- then use the following calculation:

Profit = Capital employed × Target percentage return

For example:

Capital to be employed	£50,000
Current rate of interest	10%
Provision for element of risk	20%
Target rate of return on capital employed	30%

Therefore, the minimum profit per annum required to provide a satisfactory return on capital employed in the business is:

£50,000 × 30% (30/100) = £15,000.

Sales volume, profit and cost calculations for businesses dealing in unique products

Contribution per labour hour

Many small businesses are involved in providing a unique product or service to each customer. For a plumber, no two jobs will be exactly the same – each will use up different amounts of labour and materials. This is true for many jobbing firms. In such cases, a method is required for producing estimates that will realise sufficient gross profit to cover both target net profit and overheads.

The way to proceed is to identify what factor limits your sales volume. For most service firms, this is the number of labour hours in a given period. The next step is to calculate how much gross profit will have to be generated by each labour hour to cover the target profit and fixed costs. This is a simple matter of dividing fixed costs for the period by total labour hours available:

$$\text{Contribution required from each hour} = \frac{\text{Fixed costs} + \text{Net profit target}}{\text{Total labour hours avaiable}}$$

For a garage with fixed costs of £400 (including staff pay) and a profit objective of £400 per week and 80 labour hours available, each labour hour would have to generate £10 gross profit for the business to reach breakeven. However, this assumes that all the labour hours the firm has paid staff for (assuming permanent staff are employed) have been used up, but, in most cases, this is not so. Sales will fluctuate throughout the year – some weeks may see only 70 per cent of the employees' time gainfully used. Therefore, it is safer to substitute total labour hours available for a conservative estimate of total labour hours that will be directly used in generating gross profit:

$$\text{Contribution required from each hour} = \frac{\text{Fixed costs} + \text{Net profit target}}{\text{Total labour hours used (conservative estimate)}}$$

If the previous example is reworked with a conservative estimate that, on average, only 75 per cent of the total labour hours available will be used, then the contribution required per man hour will be £13.33 (that is, £800/60 hours). On this basis, the costing for a job might look like this:

Materials	£44.50
Contribution to fixed costs and net profits,	
10 hours @ £13.33 per hour	£133.30
Total charge for job	£177.80

The price of £177.80 is that which the business would have to charge for this job to cover all costs and meet its profit goal. If this is a higher price than the customer is prepared to pay, should the business accept less to secure the order? There is no simple answer to this. The business will have to consider the following questions.

- Will turning down the job result in labour hours being idle?
- Will acceptance of the job result in profitable repeat sales?
- Will accepting the job take up slack labour hours?

If the answer to any of these questions is 'Yes', accepting the order at a lower price would probably benefit the business. The lowest price that could be accepted is one that will at least cover fixed costs. Contribution required per hour could be reduced to £400/60 hours = £6.60. The lowest possible costing would therefore be:

Materials:	£44.50
Contribution to fixed costs and net profits,	
10 hours £6.60 per hour	£66.00
Total charge for job	£110.50

Provided more profitable business is not being turned down, the logic of charging a price that does not fully contribute to desired profits is that at least it earns some money towards fixed costs. Remember, fixed costs will not change if you sell less – they will continue to build up and have to be met by your remaining sales.

■ Cost plus profit mark-up – mark-ups and margins

An alternative to the above method is to add a percentage to variable costs to obtain a selling price – this percentage is known as the mark-up. It should not be confused with the percentage profit margin. Although both refer to the same profit in money terms, in the case of profit margin the profit is expressed as a percentage of sales, whereas in the case of mark-up it is expressed as a percentage of variable cost. The actual money mark-up – that is, the gross profit – per job or unit of production, when multiplied by the number of expected sales, will, as before, have to be high enough to cover target profit and fixed costs.

To decide on what percentage mark-up to apply, you must first identify a percentage profit margin that will give you an acceptable combination of sales volume, costs and net profit. This is achieved by plotting your fixed costs on a graph and drawing in different gross profit lines based on possible percentage margins (as in Figure 6.9). When you have decided on an acceptable percentage gross margin on sales, you will need to convert this to its equivalent percentage mark-up to arrive at a selling price for each job or unit of production. The process is as follows:

$$\text{Profit margin} = \frac{\text{Profit}}{\text{Price}}$$

$$\text{Profit mark-up} = \frac{\text{Profit}}{\text{Variable cost}}$$

Then the percentage mark-up can be derived from the percentage margin by the following process:

$$\text{Profit mark-up} = \frac{\text{Profit}}{\underset{\text{(i.e. variable cost)}}{\text{Price} - \text{Profit}}} \times 100 \text{ (to turn the fraction into a percentage)}$$

The process can easily be reversed to derive a percentage margin from a percentage mark-up:

$$\text{Profit mark-up} = \frac{\text{Profit}}{\underset{\text{(i.e. price)}}{\text{Variable cost} + \text{Profit}}} \times 100 \text{ (to turn the fraction into a percentage)}$$

For example, if you decided that operating a 20 per cent gross profit margin on sales would give you the best chance of achieving your breakeven profit point, then you would have to mark your goods up by:

$$\text{Profit mark-up} = \frac{20 \text{ (profit)}}{100 \text{ (price)} - 20 \text{ (profit)}} \times 100$$

$$= \frac{20 \text{ (profit)}}{(80) \text{ (cost)}} \times 100$$

$$= 25\%$$

Margin	Mark-up	Margin	Mark-up	Margin	Mark-up
1.00%	1.01%	34.00%	51.52%	67.00%	203.03%
2.00%	2.04%	35.00%	53.85%	68.00%	212.50%
3.00%	3.09%	36.00%	56.25%	69.00%	222.58%
4.00%	4.10%	37.00%	58.73%	70.00%	233.33%
5.00%	5.26%	38.00%	61.29%	71.00%	244.83%
6.00%	6.38%	39.00%	63.93%	72.00%	257.14%
7.00%	7.53%	40.00%	66.67%	73.00%	270.37%
8.00%	8.70%	41.00%	69.49%	74.00%	284.62%
9.00%	9.89%	42.00%	72.41%	75.00%	300.00%
10.00%	11.11%	43.00%	75.44%	76.00%	316.67%
11.00%	12.36%	44.00%	78.57%	77.00%	334.78%
12.00%	13.64%	45.00%	81.82%	78.00%	354.55%
13.00%	14.94%	46.00%	85.19%	79.00%	376.19%
14.00%	16.28%	47.00%	88.68%	80.00%	400.00%
15.00%	17.75%	48.00%	92.31%	81.00%	426.32%
16.00%	19.05%	49.00%	96.08%	82.00%	455.56%
17.00%	20.48%	50.00%	100.00%	83.00%	488.24%
18.00%	21.95%	51.00%	104.08%	84.00%	525.00%
19.00%	23.46%	52.00%	108.33%	85.00%	566.67%
20.00%	25.00%	53.00%	112.77%	86.00%	614.29%
21.00%	26.58%	54.00%	117.39%	87.00%	669.23%
22.00%	28.21%	55.00%	122.22%	88.00%	733.33%
23.00%	29.87%	56.00%	127.27%	89.00%	809.09%
24.00%	31.48%	57.00%	132.56%	90.00%	900.00%
25.00%	33.33%	58.00%	138.10%	91.00%	1011.11%
26.00%	35.14%	59.00%	143.90%	92.00%	1150.00%
27.00%	36.99%	60.00%	150.00%	93.00%	1328.57%
28.00%	38.89%	61.00%	156.41%	94.00%	1566.67%
29.00%	40.95%	62.00%	163.16%	95.00%	1900.00%
30.00%	42.86%	63.00%	170.27%	96.00%	2400.00%
31.00%	44.93%	64.00%	177.78%	97.00%	3233.33%
32.00%	47.06%	65.00%	185.71%	98.00%	4900.00%
33.00%	49.25%	66.00%	194.12%	99.00%	9900.00%
				100.00%	

Fig. 6.10 Conversion chart from gross margin to mark-up

To help you check your calculations, refer to the conversion chart in Figure 6.10.

The final step is to apply this mark-up to a range of jobs or products to check whether or not it will result in competitive prices.

THE PROJECTED PROFIT AND LOSS ACCOUNT

Having detailed and classified all of your costs, decided on a selling price(s) and arrived at a breakeven profit point to give you the necessary sales volume to achieve your net profit goal, you are ready to compile a summary of the expected profit position of your business at the end of its first year's trading. This summary is known as a profit and loss account. In its simplest form, it shows the expected sales revenue and details of total costs that have been incurred within the trading year. The costs are subtracted from the sales revenue to give the gross and net profits. It is laid out as shown in the example given in Figure 6.11.

	£	£
Sales		100,000
Stock costs (net of closing stock):	75,000	
Gross profit		25,000
Overheads		
Rent	4,000	
Utilities	2,000	
Advertising	3,000	
Professional fees	1,500	
General expenses	1,500	
	12,000	
Net profit before tax		13,000

Fig. 6.11 Projecting and compiling a profit and loss account

The sales revenue is taken directly from the BEPP. If your BEPP is physical units of production, then obviously sales volume will have to be multiplied by selling price to obtain sales revenue.

The cost of stock sold is the variable cost in this case. If variable costs have been plotted on a breakeven chart, the figure is simply read off the chart. If a percentage margin has been used to arrive at BEPP, then the percentage of sales revenue that is variable cost will be 100 (sales revenue or selling price) minus the profit margin. For example, if the profit margin is 25 per cent then the cost of goods must be 75 per cent of the sales revenue.

The fixed costs are simply entered from your estimates.

SUMMARY

Detailing and classifying the costs of your business and examining the way in which they interact with sales volume and selling price is the key to establishing the profit or loss it may make. It is a major part of the planning process for any new business venture and should be carried out with as much accuracy as possible. Once completed, it should be referred to constantly as the business grows; comparison of projected and actual costs should be monitored closely and acted on as necessary.

The results of your costing exercise may require you to carry out further market research or even revise the nature of your business venture. Do not become disheartened by this, for the costing will have served its purpose in preventing you from making costly, maybe ruinous, mistakes.

If the conclusion from your work in this chapter is that your business venture will make a profit, do not automatically assume the business is viable, for you might not be able to finance its overall capital requirements.

Checklist

1 Do you know the difference between cost and capital?

2 Have you made a full assessment of all of your fixed costs, including:
- depreciation
- interest charges
- administration
- production
- selling (including advertising budget)
- maintenance and repairs
- utilities, telephone, electricity, gas and water
- transport
- miscellaneous budget
- full cost of permanent staff
- professional fees (accountant/solicitor)?

3 Can any of your fixed costs be reduced by:

- delaying purchases

- buying second-hand?

4 Are all of your fixed costs necessary?

5 Have you compared the cost of leasing fixed assets to outright purchase?

6. Have you made a full assessment of your variable costs?

7. Have you researched suppliers of stock, equipment and services fully ?

8 Have you chosen your suppliers of stock, equipment and services on some objective basis, such as:
- delivery times;
- price;
- discount terms on bulk purchases;
- delivery cost;
- payment terms;
- quality and reliability?

9 How will the work be organised?

10 Can you reduce your variable costs by organising production, selling or administration better?

11 Have you estimated your target profit?

12 Does it allow for a satisfactory rate of return on the capital employed in your business?

13 Does it allow for retaining profits in the business to finance future trading?

14 What is your breakeven sales figure – your best and worst estimates?

15 What is your breakeven profit sales figure, best and worst estimate?

16 Does your market research information confirm that your breakeven figures are achievable?

17 What margin of safety have you allowed?

18 Are your costings too optimistic?

19 If necessary, have you selected and used an appropriate method for compiling job estimates?

20 Do you know the difference between a percentage margin and a percentage mark-up?

21 Have you compiled a projected profit and loss account to show the expected position at the end of your first year's trading?

How much capital will you need?

1
2
3
4
5
6

7

8
9
10

INTRODUCTION

One of the commonest mistakes made by potential new businesses is getting the total money/capital requirements for efficiently starting up and operating their new venture wrong – you can't afford to make such a mistake.

The actual amount you need will, of course, vary with the scale and nature of your business, but all businesses will have to find capital for two specific purposes.

- The acquisition of items the business expects to keep for a long period of time (that is, for periods greater than a year) such as premises and equipment – these are known as fixed assets and 'accordingly' the capital necessary to acquire them is known as fixed capital.
- The provision of sufficient monies to operate the business on a day-to-day basis. This is known as working capital and is needed to cover payments for such items as stock, materials and pay that are regular outgoings throughout the trading year. This capital is constantly 'working' to keep the business alive.

Together, the capital requirements in each of these areas will represent the total amount of money you will need to invest in the business at any one time. The best way forward is to examine each broad area of capital requirements in turn.

WHAT FIXED ASSETS WILL YOUR BUSINESS NEED?

Nearly all businesses will require a certain amount of fixed capital. For many, the acquisition of premises will represent the largest fixed capital investment they will make, and partly for this reason, this is dealt with in a chapter of its own. For some small service businesses operating from home (say, mobile hairdressing), fixed capital expenditure could be low, consisting perhaps of a few items of inexpensive equipment and a second-hand car. Different businesses will require different fixed assets to make the manufacture or provision of their end product or service possible. An example of a possible fixed asset requirement schedule for a small retail business is given in Figure 7.1.

	Investments (£)
Premises (leasehold, 185 square metres	18,000
Shop frontage sign and decor	2,500
Display stands and shelving	3,000
Freezer display units	1,750
Chiller display units	1,750
Cold storage	1,000
Pricing guns (2)	120
Trolleys and baskets	300
Miscellaneous equipment	200
Electronic till	700
Computer (accounts/stock control)	1,200
Small delivery van	7,500
	38,020

Fig. 7.1 Fixed assets for a small food shop

A number of factors will influence your decisions as to what items you should acquire and on what scale. These can be roughly listed under the following headings.

- **The market for your business** You will have to acquire assets that are consistent in their attributes with the needs of your customers.
- **The nature of your product/service** Obviously, each product and service will need different assets to make its manufacture/selling and distribution as attractive to customers as possible.
- **The goals of your business** Your 'shopping list' for fixed assets must be consistent with what you intend your business to achieve in terms of its markets, profitability and organisation. It is certainly a good idea to list your business' goals along with their separate resource/asset requirements. For example, if the goal is reducing shoplifting to 2 per cent of sales achieving it would require an effective surveillance and security system, possibly implying the necessity of such assets as closed-circuit TV surveillance and security mirrors.
- **The scale of finance at your disposal** Most small businesses, and even SMEs, have limited finance available with which to pur-

chase assets. In effect, there will be competition between various investment proposals for this limited finance. In deciding whether or not to acquire any fixed asset you should ask yourself the following questions.

– What will it do for my business?
– Is it really needed?
– Will the acquisition of the asset prevent the business from acquiring other assets? If so, what effect would that have on the business?

– Is there an alternative item available that will achieve similar ends? If so, which will represent the most cost-effective purchase?

Carefully consider the effect these factors will have on your requirements and compile your fixed asset list.

HOW MUCH WORKING CAPITAL WILL YOUR BUSINESS NEED?

■ The circulation of working capital

Clearly, fixed capital will stay 'locked up' in fixed assets for a long time. Working capital is more 'liquid' in that it changes its form more rapidly. To illustrate this, look at the way working capital circulates in a small manufacturing business, McKenzie Limited, shown in Figure 7.2. Money goes out to buy materials, services and labour needed to produce and sell the finished product, and eventually money comes back as customers pay cash. Following the cycle through, working capital changes from money into raw materials, then into partly finished goods (inclusive of the conversion costs: rates, pay, electricity, and so on), then into stocks of finished products, then into 30-day loans made to customers who have bought the products under such payment terms, and then finally back into cash as the customers settle their accounts. In our example, on any given day, there will be money in the bank (or there should be if the business is to

> *Clearly, fixed capital will stay 'locked up' in fixed assets for a long time. Working capital is more 'liquid'.*

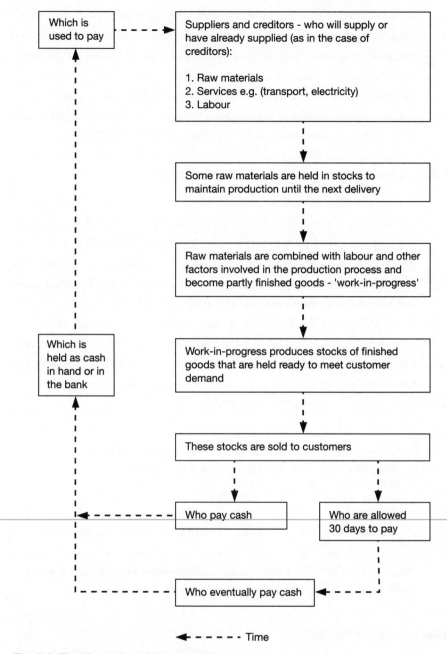

Fig. 7.2 The flow of working capital

remain solvent) to meet outgoings for supplies, pay and other expenses, stocks of raw materials, work-in-progress and finished products, cash coming in from sales and money owing to the business from customers who have not yet settled their accounts. All these items represent things that the business possesses – they are its current assets. Being differentiated from its fixed assets in that they will be turned back into cash, hopefully, in the near future.

■ Gross working capital and current assets

For an existing business, if you add up the total value of its current assets on any one day, you will have calculated its total gross working capital. To illustrate, the calculation of McKenzie Limited's gross working capital on 3 August 1988 is shown in Figure 7.3. However, what is very important to note is that that is the total gross working capital requirements at 3 August 1988 and that more working capital may be required a day, a week or a month later. For instance, if McKenzie Limited plans to increase sales, then it is obvious that more working capital will have to be invested in the full range of its current assets to make those sales possible.

	£	
Cash in hand	1,500	(ready to pay suppliers
Raw materials	3,000	and expenses)
Work-in-progress	2,500	
Finished products	1,500	
Debtors	700	(total value of customer accounts
Gross working capital	9,200	outstanding on 3 August 1988)

Fig. 7.3 Total gross working capital on McKenzie Limited on 3 August 1988

■ Net working capital

In case you were beginning to worry that you will have to fund all the gross working capital requirements of your business, you may now sigh with relief, as that is not the case. Just as businesses have things that they possess – assets – they also have things that they owe

– liabilities. Short-term liabilities such as trade credit and overdrafts – known as current liabilities – reduce the working capital that has to be found from the internal resources of the business (or, if you prefer simpler terminology, 'from your own pocket'). The difference between current assets and current liabilities is the amount your business will have to contribute to gross working capital. This is known as net working capital.

Obtaining interest-free trade credit (usually 30 days) is the best method of reducing net working capital requirements. For example, imagine a business with no current asset requirements other than stock, that can obtain 30 days credit from its supplier and sell all that stock within 28 days of receipt. It would have net working capital requirements of nil. In effect, the supplier of the goods would be funding all the gross working capital requirements for free. However, in reality, this is rarely the case. A business operating in such a way may, in fact, expose itself to severe cash flow problems if it fails to turn its stock into cash in sufficient time to meet the payment deadline (see Cash flows on page 161).

Obtaining interest-free trade credit (usually 30 days) is the best method of reducing net working capital requirements.

■ Calculating your working capital requirements

The working capital your business will require at any one time is dependent on:

- the length of time it will take for the working capital to complete the cycle from cash to stocks and back into cash again;
- the level of sales it has to support.

The longer it takes to complete the cycle and the higher your level of sales, the more gross working capital you will need to run the business.

Let us examine the commonest current assets you might have to fund – stock and debtors, including how to establish/calculate their individual working capital requirements. The other major current asset all businesses require is cash. This subject warrants lengthy discussion and will be dealt with separately.

■ *Stock*

If you hold stocks of finished goods or raw materials, you will have to solve the problem of how big those stocks will have to be. The two main factors that will affect the size of your stocks are:

- the usage rate – the daily, weekly or monthly rate at which finished goods are sold or raw materials consumed by the production process;
- the lead time between placing an order and receiving the goods or the time lapses between deliveries.

The weekly time lapses between deliveries, multiplied by the weekly usage rate, plus a margin of safety will determine the necessary maximum stock level to maintain the business. The smaller the time lapse between deliveries, the smaller the working capital that is required for stock. The example in Figure 7.4 clearly shows this relationship.

When stocks are at a maximum just after delivery, XYZ enjoys the benefit of operating with £4000 less working capital than ABC due to the simple fact that it has secured more frequent supplies. Effectively, this means that XYZ has a faster cycle of working capital. ABC has to wait four weeks to realise the full return on the capital it has invested whereas XYZ only has to wait two weeks.

It is impossible to make any general rules about the minimum stock levels you must hold – each business will have its own peculiarities. Suffice it to say that when compiling an estimate, you should carefully assess customer demand. For instance, what breadth and depth of stocks will they demand you to have on hand or display? The greater your stock range, the greater your minimum stock level will have to be.

An alternative or complementary way to estimate your average stock requirements is to refer to the average rate of stock-turn for your type and size of business in published statistics. The rate of stock-turn figure is the number of times the average holding of stock has been sold in a given period of time (usually one year). It is obtained by the simple formula shown in Figure 7.5.

	ABC Ltd	XYZ Ltd
Weekly sales @ cost (i.e. usage rate of stock)	£2,000	£2,000
Lead time in weeks	4×	2×
Value of reorder to maintain stocks	£8,000	£4,000
	+	+
Minimum safety stocks held	£1,000	£1,000
Maximum stock level	£9,000	£5,000

Fig. 7.4 The effect of different lead times on stock level

Rate of stock-turn = $\dfrac{\text{Value of the volume of sales for the period}}{\text{Value of average stock level}}$

(*Note:* both sales and stock should be at the same valuation. For example, if the stock level is valued at cost price so must the sales volume.)

Fig. 7.5 Calculation of rate of stock-turn

The rate of stock-turn (RST) is in effect a measure of how long stocks are held for and, consequently, the circulation speed of working capital in the business – the more frequently stock is turned over (bought and sold), the less working capital is required to finance stocks. An RST of 52 per annum means that one week's stock is on hand; an RST of 12 per annum means that a month's stock is held, and so on.

If you know what rate of stock-turn you can reasonably expect for your type and scale of business and your estimated sales for your first year's trading (from market research see Chapter 3), then it is a relatively easy matter to calculate/estimate the amount of working capital you will have tied up in stocks and for how long. For instance, if you were planning to open a newsagent's with an estimated RST of 5.6 and projected sales of £120,000 per annum, then you could reasonably expect that:

- on average, you will have to hold 65 days' worth of stock, because stock is expected to be turned over 5.6 times in the year – 365/5.6 = 65;
- the retail value of that stock will be £21,370: (65/365) × £120,000 = £21,370 (on average);
- if the margin of profit on that stock is 36 per cent, then the valuation at cost will be £13,677, because 100 per cent = retail value, 36 per cent = profit, cost = 100 per cent – 36 per cent, therefore 64 per cent of £21,370 (21,370 × 64/100) = £13,677.

The method to use to estimate how much working capital (on average) you will have tied up in stock is simplified in Figure 7.6. The method for calculating a day's stock is simplified in Figure 7.7.

$$\text{Average stock level} = \frac{\text{Value of the volume of sales for the period}}{\text{Rate of stock-turn}}$$

Note: If you use a sales estimate valued at selling price then the value of average stock you obtain will also be at selling price. Thus, to revalue the stock at cost price (i.e. what you will pay for it), you have to reduce its value by your expected gross profit percentage margin. (For a full discussion of gross profit and the calculation of percentage margins, see Chapter 6.)

Fig. 7.6 Calculation of average stock requirements for a given level of sales using annual rate of stock-turn

---

$$\text{Days' stock held} = \frac{\text{Value of average stock level}}{\text{Value of volume of sales per annum}} \times 365 \text{ (days in period)}$$

Note: Both sales and stock should be at the same valuation, either cost or selling price. If you want to compare days' stock held to days' credit given by your suppliers you should value both sales and stock at cost.

Fig. 7.7 Calculation of days' stock held

If you expect to secure trade credit, it is useful to compare the number of days credit is given (on average) by your suppliers to the number of days stock is held (on average) to estimate your average net working capital requirements for stock. If the newsagent's in the previous example could secure 30-day trade credit, then it would effectively reduce the time average stocks are held from 65 to 35 days. The business would only have to finance 35 days' worth of stock instead of 65. Hence, the net working capital required to finance its average stockholding would decrease from £13,677 to £7,365 – that is (35/65) × £13,677 thus:

Assets		
	Stock	£13,677
Liabilities		
	Creditor	£6,312
	Net working capital	£7,365

Exercise Try to find out the information on working capital requirements for stock from one of the following sources.

- Trade magazines, trade associations, government statistics, talking to people in your line of business.
- Obtain copies of final accounts of businesses for sale that are similar to the type you intend to set up. The accounts should contain the necessary information, sales and stock figures, for you to use the formula given in Figure 7.5 to calculate the business' rate of stock-turn. Calculate the RST for a number of businesses, take an average and apply it to your venture.

If you are going to be involved in manufacturing or providing a service that involves 'adding value' to raw materials, then don't forget your 'stocks' will consist of raw materials, work-in-progress (WIP) and finished goods. Raw materials will be valued at the cost price of their purchase, but WIP and finished goods will have labour and overhead costs 'stored up' in them (look again at the cycle of working capital in Figure 7.2). Consequently, the valuation of WIP and finished goods stocks must be inclusive of the conversion costs. To

Raw materials	£
Three weeks stock (3/52 × £50 000)	2885
WIP: two weeks' stock	
raw material content (2/52 × £50 000)	1923
labour and overhead content ([2/52 × £40 000]/2)	769

(As each stage of the production process is expected to use (absorb) equal proportions of overhead and labour expenses, the value of these expenses used (absorbed) by the WIP is averaged at half the total cost of converting raw materials to finished products.)

Finished products	
two weeks' stock (2/52 × £90 000)	3462
gross going capital required	9038

Fig. 7.8 Projection of HS Alarms' gross working capital requirements

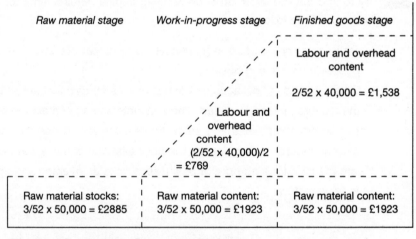

Fig. 7.9 HS Alarms' working capital cycle

estimate working capital requirements in such a case will therefore require a detailed breakdown of unit costs (see Chapter 6) in addition to projecting the average number of days each category of stocks will be held.

The following example illustrates how to calculate the working capital requirements for the three types of stock to achieve a given sales target.

HS Alarms is a new business planning to manufacture and sell home security systems. In its first year, it expects to achieve sales of 10,000 units. The detailed breakdown of costs to achieve this level of sales is as follows.

	£
Materials	50,000
Labour	20,000
Overheads	20,000
	90,000
Profit	10,000
	100,000

HS Alarms has also projected that:

- it will have to hold raw material stocks representing three weeks' usage (based on a combination of the minimum size of an economic reorder quantity and lead time);
- WIP will take two weeks to pass through the production process;
- it will have to hold two weeks' stock of finished security systems to meet the market's need for immediate delivery.

To aid financial planning, HS Alarms need to calculate the amount of working capital that will be required to fund stocks of raw materials, WIP and finished products. The calculation is shown in Figure 7.8 and the working capital cycle clearly illustrated in Figure 7.9.

■ Debtors

Selling on credit lengthens the working capital cycle and thereby increases the amount of working capital required to operate the business.

For instance, if HS Alarms was to offer 30 days' settlement terms to all its customers, it would increase its gross working capital requirements (on average) by £7397 (30/365 days × £90,000). However, allowing for slow payers, the actual length of credit taken would probably be 45 days, a substantial increase of £11,096 (45/365 days × £90,000).

If you plan to sell on credit, work out the greatest and least demands credit sales will make on working capital. As a general guide to working out the lengths of credit your customers will take, increase the days' credit allowed by at least a half to account for slow payers. If you are going to sell to other businesses, find out how fast they usually settle their accounts. You will probably discover that many companies (particularly the larger ones) will think nothing of taking up to three months to pay. Failure now to investigate the days' credit your potential customers may take will probably spell disaster for you in the future.

HOW MUCH CASH WILL YOUR BUSINESS NEED?

■ Cash, profit and capital

It is not uncommon for newcomers to business to mistake cash for profit. Cash and profit are two distinct terms. Cash can come from a variety of sources – loans, overdrafts, retained profits and so on. Profits come from the difference between a business revenue and its costs.

If a business is undercapitalised (that is, it does not have enough capital to cover fixed assets and working capital), then part or all of the profits will have to be retained to make up the shortfall. Profits will then be tied up financing such items as equipment, stocks, bills that have to be paid in advance, debtors and so on. It can be seen from this that

> *It is not uncommon for newcomers to business to mistake cash for profit.*

profit does not necessarily take the form of a growing bank balance. Consequently, a business can be making a healthy profit but be overdrawn at the bank. This position is fine if it is controlled, planned for and temporary – it is when it becomes uncontrolled, unplanned and permanent that disaster strikes. Cash is the lifeblood of a business and without it new materials, pay, stock and so on cannot be financed.

■ Cash flows

You should now be fully familiar with the idea that working capital circulates in the business and, as it does so, it changes form – from cash to stock to debtors to cash. Cash, as part of the cycle, flows into and out of the business. For a business to continue trading, there must be more cash coming in (from whatever source) than going out – otherwise, it will be unable to meet its liabilities (debts) and become insolvent. If the owner of such a business continues to trade knowing that such a situation exists, then they will be liable to prosecution for fraudulent trading. At the very least, creditors will make claims in law against such a business and these could lead to bankruptcy.

To minimise the risk of insolvency, all businesses should forecast their cash needs. Before you start your business, you must prepare what is known as a cash flow forecast for your first year's trading. This is a month-by-month or week-by-week forecast of how much cash will be coming in and how much will be going out. To some extent you probably already do this with your own personal finances, but in a less formal way. 'If Bob pays me back that money he owes me on time and I get that tax rebate, I should be able to cover the electricity bill at the end of the month ... but how am I going to find enough cash for the holiday the following month ... I wonder if I will get that pay rise?'

To draw up a cash flow forecast you will need to know:

- how much cash is coming in, when and from where;
- how much cash is going out, when and where to.

Exercise Before you attempt to do this for your business idea, compile a cash flow forecast for your own personal or family finances – this will help you understand the process involved.

■ Forecasting personal and family cash needs

Exercise First, prepare a list of cash in and cash out, as in the examples in Figure 7.10 and then use this information to compile a cash flow forecast as in Figure 7.11.

Cash in

Item	When received	Comments
David's pay	monthly	£600 net, increases to £650 in September
Sue's pay	weekly	part-time shop worker, with extra hours during the summer and Christmas period

Cash out

Item	When received	Comments
Mortgage	monthly	£175 per month
Life assurance	monthly	£40 per month
Loan	monthly	£38 per month
Gas	quarterly	use previous years' bills and allow for price increases and extra appliances
Electricity	quarterly	as above
Telephone	quarterly	previous bills show little change over the year
Water rates	half year	£53 in October; £63 in April
House insurance	quarterly	£28 per quarter
TV licence	per annum	£55
Car tax	half year	£55
Car insurance	per annum	£100
Petrol	–	£48 per month
Clothes	–	new clothes for holidays and school clothes for children in September
Food	–	£180 per month
Miscellaneous	–	£100 per month – general expenses
Holidays	–	£280
Christmas	–	£200 presents, etc.

Fig. 7.10 Personal cash budget

	July	Aug	Sept	Oct	Nov	Dec	Jan	Feb	Mar	April	May	June	Totals
Cash in													
Pay 1	600	600	650	650	650	650	650	650	650	650	650	650	7,700
Pay 2	200	200	100	100	100	320	80	80	80	80	80	130	1,550
Total cash in	800	800	750	750	750	970	730	730	730	730	730	780	9,250
Cash out													
Mortgage	175	175	175	175	175	175	175	175	175	175	175	175	2,100
Life assurance	40	40	40	40	40	40	40	40	40	40	40	40	480
Credit cards	28	28	28	28	28	28	28	28	28	28	28	28	336
Rates	42	42	42	42	42	42	42	42	42	42	42	42	504
Bank loan	38	38	38	38	38	38	38	38	38	38	38	38	456
Gas			30			50			50			40	170
Electricity			60			90			90			60	300
Telephone		47			47			47			47		188
Water rates		28			28			28			28		112
House insurance				53						63			116
TV licence							55						55
Car tax				55						55			110
Car ins				100									100
Petrol	48	48	48	48	48	48	48	48	48	48	48	48	576
Clothes		100				100							200
Food	180	180	180	180	180	180	180	180	180	180	180	180	2,160
Miscellaneous	40	40	40	40	40	40	40	40	40	40	40	40	480
Misc		20	20	20	20	20	20	20	20	20	20	20	220
Holiday		280											280
Christmas						300							300
Total cash out	591	1,066	701	819	686	1,151	666	686	751	729	686	711	9,243
Monthly balance	209	(266)	49	(69)	64	(181)	64	44	(21)	1	44	69	7
Opening balance	0	209	(57)	(8)	(77)	(13)	(194)	(130)	(86)	(107)	(106)	(62)	
Closing balance (Cumulative)	209	(57)	(8)	(77)	(13)	(194)	(130)	(86)	(107)	(106)	(62)	7	

Fig. 7.11 Personal cash flow forecast

The top of the cash flow forecast shows the cash coming in – in the example, David's and Sue's pay. The middle section shows the cash going out each month; and the bottom half shows the all-important monthly cash balances. The first balance shows the surplus (or deficit in brackets) for each month (total cash in minus total cash out). The second is the opening balance for the month (the closing balance from the previous month brought forward). The third is the closing balance (the cumulative cash position, calculated by adding the monthly cash surplus or deficit to the opening balance for the month).

David's and Sue's cash flow forecast shows that they will need to obtain an overdraft from the bank for the greater part of the year or attempt to reduce expenditure on some items if possible. The main cause of their shortage of cash is the planned expenditure on a holiday in August. As their total cash flows in only exceed total cash flows out by £7 over the course of the year, perhaps it would be wise for them to forgo the holiday this year. Whatever they decide, they now have useful information and a good method at their disposal to look into the future, know when problems are on the way and be able to take action to prevent them.

■ Forecasting cash needs for a business start-up

Compiling a cash flow forecast for a new business is similar to the exercise you have just carried out for your personal or family cash needs. The difference will be in where the cash comes from and where it goes to. There will also be a greater degree of difficulty in estimating the timing and volume of the cash inflows and outflows. Let's look at cash in and cash out in turn and then consider a fully worked example.

■ *Cash in*

Cash coming into a business comes from a number of sources: sales, owner's capital and loan capital.

Sales

Ideally any businessperson would like to see their sales evenly spread out over the year. Clearly this would make the business easier to plan and operate. However, depending on the nature of the market for your business (see Chapter 3) your sales pattern will probably fluctuate.

The first task, then, is to translate your sales pattern into an estimate of monthly sales. How you do this will depend on the nature of the information gained from your market research and the level of detail.

If all of your sales are on a cash basis, then the pattern of your cash inflows will be the same as your sales pattern. However, if your business will sell all or part of its products/services on a credit basis, then the cash from those sales will lag behind the actual sales by the average number of days of credit taken by your customers. For example, if you are offering one month's settlement terms, then the cash from sales made in January will not come in until February, perhaps even later when you account for slow payers (as noted earlier in the chapter).

How accurate your sales projections will be depends on the number and nature of assumptions you have to make. Obviously, nobody can predict the future with 100 per cent accuracy, so golden rules in compiling a cash flow projection are to:

- underestimate cash coming in from sales;
- overestimate cash going out.

It is better to be pleasantly surprised by having more cash than expected than having to face an unexpected cash crisis six months after you have started.

Capital

To start the business, it is obvious that a certain amount of money has to be put in to finance a variety of purchases so that sales can be generated. There will be injections of capital. These will either come from your own personal funds or from long- or short-term loans (see Chapter 8). You can obtain an approximation of the amount of capital you will have to find by adding together your estimates of fixed and average working capital requirements for your first year. However, this will not be entirely accurate because it will not take into account or include:

- variations in working capital requirements associated with fluctuating sales over time;
- the timing of your fixed asset purchases;
- the size and timings of your own personal drawings from the business.

You can, of course, calculate your exact working capital requirements for each monthly or weekly period. However, this can prove rather tedious. The compilation of the cash flow will help you to decide the actual size, timing and nature of the capital injections you will have to put into the business. A simple method is to draw up a 'first' cash flow forecast without any capital input, then substitute different scales and timings of capital injections until a satisfactory cumulative cash flow position is reached. As this indicates the cash flow forecast, it is an ideal tool for solving 'If ...?' -type problems. For example, if I increase the initial capital input by £2000, what effect will that have on my cumulative cash flow in month four?'

■ *Cash out*

Cash outflows will result from expenditure on:

- fixed costs (overheads), such as rent, rates, electricity and so on;
- variable or direct costs – for most, this will be mainly stock;
- fixed asset purchases, such as premises and equipment;
- personal drawings;
- loan repayments (net of interest);
- taxation payments.

Overheads

These are the easiest to predict because, by definition, they are not affected by short-term fluctuations in sales (see Chapter 6). You will have to research in detail the timings of such payments. Here is a rough guide.

- Utilities, such as electricity and gas, are paid quarterly in arrears. However, it is possible you may have to pay connection charges or a deposit if you are a new customer. If you wish to spread the costs more evenly over time, you can have your future bills estimated and arrange for monthly payments to be made direct from your bank account.

■ Rent is usually paid in advance. The terms of leases vary, but it is not uncommon to pay quarterly or six-monthly in advance.

■ Buildings and contents insurance is usually paid for in advance. However, most insurance companies will usually arrange monthly payments.

■ Pay is usually given to staff a week or a month in arrears. It is obviously better to pay monthly than weekly as this shortens the net working capital cycle. PAYE and NI deductions from pay will be paid monthly in arrears. Therefore, net pay (that is, after deductions) should be shown separately on the cash flow forecast.

■ Advertising budget – if you intend to promote your business effectively you will have to compile a sales promotion plan (Chapter 4 tells you how to do it). Such a plan should also contain the size and timing of the costs involved.

■ Motor vehicle expenses – road tax and insurance can be readily estimated; petrol with a little more difficulty. The main problem is with unexpected expenditure on such items as repairs and so on. One way to account for the unexpected is to allocate a sum to a contingency fund for such eventualities. Another is to lease the vehicle (the lease to cover repairs and so on) or to take out a maintenance contract that includes regular servicing and breakdowns – this is equally applicable to other forms of equipment and machinery.

■ Professional fees – expenditure on legal and accountancy services will undoubtedly be erratic. You will perhaps make more use of such services in the initial start-up period and at the end of your trading year as your final accounts are drawn up than at other times.

■ Miscellaneous items, includes expenditure on numerous minor items, such as coffee, stationery, cleaning materials and so on. For cash flow purposes, it is better to put the same amount down each month.

Variable costs

These, by definition, will vary with sales. Therefore, in the first instance, the accuracy of predicted cash outflows related to variable costs will directly depend on the accuracy of monthly sales estimates. For many businesses, the largest single item representing continuous cash outflows is stock purchase. Much has already been said about stocks; detailed consideration must also be given to:

- the size of initial stock;
- the frequency with which stocks will be replaced;
- the payment terms.

Initial stocks Calculating the size of the initial stock level can prove a problem. For a retail business, the simplest method is to use the annual rate of stock-turn (as discussed earlier). For example, if the expected rate of stock-turn is 12 and the projected sales are £120,000, then the initial stocks will be £10,000 at retail prices. However, this method neglects the fact that sales will vary from month to month and will probably be well below the norm in the first few months of trading, resulting in too much stock being carried when sales are low.

A refinement is to apply the RST per annum as a ratio of stock to sales for the sales pattern over a shorter term, say two or three months. For example, a business with an expected RST of 12 per annum and sales of £18,000 for the first quarter would require initial stocks of £6,000.

Neither method is perfect, so you may quite legitimately choose a compromise between the two or some alternative method based on detailed knowledge of the stock requirements of your particular business.

Frequency of deliveries The more often a business can obtain deliveries, the fewer days, weeks or months in advance it has to buy stock. A business that only receives deliveries every two months faces the situation of having stock to sell in March that was delivered in January. In times of rapid expansion, this can cause severe cash flow problems as stocks have to be built up rapidly from relatively low cash inflows.

Payment terms If a business has to pay cash on delivery, then purchases in any one month will have to be paid for in that month. However, if a business can secure, for example, one month's credit, then January's purchases will not show on the cash flow forecast until February, February's until March, and so on. Therefore, the impact of poor delivery frequencies on the cash flow can be lessened by securing trade credit.

Capital expenditure

For your major purchases (fixed assets), you must draw up a detailed schedule of amounts and timings of payments. This is simple to do and, like most people, you will probably find that most of this expenditure will occur in the pre-start-up period of the business.

Personal drawings

This has nothing to do with profits. Quite simply, it is the amount you will draw from the business to finance your personal needs. The best way to estimate this is to draw up your own personal cash flow forecast as suggested earlier.

Loan repayments

Like most businesses, you will have to borrow money and, consequently, there will be loan repayments. These will include both capital and interest repayments. As far as the profit and loss account is concerned, the interest will be charged as a cost and the capital repayments will come out of profits, but for the cash flow forecast, no distinction need be made. Remember that the cash flow forecast is only concerned with cash in and out.

You may not know exactly how much you will need to borrow until you have compiled your first cash flow projection. You can make the necessary adjustments later.

Overdraft interest and bank charges

You will not know the size of the overdraft you will require until you have completed your first cash flow. Let the bank do the calculations for you and then make the necessary adjustments to the cash flow forecast.

Taxation

Depending on the nature and scale of your business, you may pay taxes to the Inland Revenue, National Insurance (NI) contributions (for your employees and yourself) and value added tax (VAT). Similar taxes to VAT are found in the USA, such as sales and inventory taxes, which vary from state to state and county to county. American readers are well advised to contact their local tax collector's office for full information on such taxes in their locality and then carefully examine the effect(s) they may have on cash flow.

■ A cash flow example

Important note: To make the following example realistic VAT has been included. However, the assumption is made that all supplies (with the exception of business rates and insurance) are subject to VAT at the standard rate of 17.5%. In preparing your forecasts you must identify which items in your business are liable for VAT and at what rate. You should note that the regulations governing VAT are complicated so you should clarify any doubts you have about it with your local VAT office or accountant. (If you have access to the Internet, connection guides to VAT, IR and NI can be found on the Internet at the web site www.open.gov.uk.) To prevent over-complexity, PAYE and NI contributions have not been included – you should, of course, include these payments as appropriate in your cash flow projections.

Susan has decided to start a business, called OneShop, with £70,000 of her own capital. She has carefully researched the market for her business and the costs involved and put together the following information on which she has based her cash flow forecast in Figure 7.13 (see later).

Sales

Figure 7.12 shows the breakdown of OneShop's sales for the first 12 months. OneShop will allow one month's credit to customers: so, for example, August's credit sales will be received in September, cash from September's sales in October and so on.

All cash in from sales will be shown inclusive of VAT.

Purchases

The business expects to operate on a 30% profit margin. Therefore, the cost of stock purchases should be 70% of the selling price.

The business is expected to have an annual rate of stock-turn of six (two months' stock will be held on average). This means that an opening stock will be needed to support the first two months' trading, August and September. August and September's sales total £63,945 (at retail prices excluding VAT) therefore an opening stock of £44,762 at cost excluding VAT (ie reduced by the 30% margin, 70/100 x £63,945) will be required. The actual cash out flow on this stock will include VAT, so the amount included in the cash flow will be £52,595. On this basis, the purchasing budget over the course of the year is projected as in Figure 7.12

Purchases will be paid for cash on delivery. After month six, one month's credit will given by suppliers of stock. Therefore, there will be no cash outflow on stock purchases in February.

Overheads

Item	Cost per annum £	Inc VAT £	Month £	Quarter £	Notes
Shop rental	20,000	23,500	—	5,875	Quarterly, in advance
Rates	1,200	—	100	—	Monthly
Utilities	6,000	7,050	—	1,763	Quarterly, in arrears
Insurance	2,000	—	—	—	Annual in advance
Van lease	3,000	3,525	294	—	Monthly
Petrol	2,000	2,350	196	—	Monthly
Expenses	2,400	2,820	235	—	Monthly
Advertising	6,000	7,050	588	—	£2,350 in Aug, Dec and April
Legal start-up	1,000	1,175	98	—	Legal and financial services
Legal/Accounts	2,000	2,350	196	—	VAT returns
Total:	45,600				

171

Capital expenditure

Item	Cost £	Timing	Plus VAT £
Electronic till	1,000	On start-up	1,175
Display equipment	2,000	On start-up	2,350
Storage equipment	1,000	On start-up	1,175
Subtotal	4,000	On start-up	4,700
Second till	1,000	In December	1,175
Total:	5,000		5,875

VAT

Susan has agreed to submit her VAT return every quarter, in arrears. The first return will be due at the beginning of November.

The business will pay VAT (at 17.5%) on purchases of stock and most of the overhead costs (as noted above) and fixed assets (as noted above) and charge VAT at the same rate on sales.

The estimated VAT payable to, or refundable from, Customs and Excise at the end of each quarter is calculated by subtracting the VAT payable on purchases of stock and fixed assets (input tax) from that charged on invoiced sales (output tax). The sales forecast (Figure 7.12) is used to calculate the total quarterly output tax collected or due (in the case of credit sales). The schedule of monthly stock purchases is used to calculate the total quarterly input tax paid or due to be paid (in the case of purchases acquired on credit after February). Note that even though the payment for stocks received in February will not be due until March, the delivery will be invoiced in February.

The calculation of the VAT payable or refundable for each quarter is shown on page 175. To arrive at the VAT figure for each quarter the output tax is subtracted from the input tax. If the business has paid more VAT than it has collected then a refund will be due (as is the case in November).

Sales pattern

	Cash sales		Credit sales		Total sales	
	ex. VAT	plus VAT	ex. VAT	plus VAT	ex. VAT	plus VAT
August	14,400	16,920	16,920	19,881	31,320	36,801
September	15,000	17,625	17,625	20,709	32,625	38,334
October	15,900	18,683	18,683	21,952	34,583	40,634
November	16,800	19,740	19,740	23,195	36,540	42,935
December	20,400	23,970	23,970	28,165	44,370	52,135
January	15,300	17,978	17,978	21,124	33,278	39,101
February	15,000	17,625	17,625	20,709	32,625	38,334
March	18,600	21,855	21,855	25,680	40,455	47,535
April	19,800	23,265	23,265	27,336	43,065	50,601
May	21,000	24,675	24,675	28,993	45,675	53,668
June	21,000	24,675	24,675	28,993	45,675	53,668
July	21,300	25,028	25,028	29,407	46,328	54,435
	214,500	252,038	252,038	296,144	466,538	548,182

Stock purchasing budget

	Sales	Stock @ retail ex. VAT	Stock @ cost ex. VAT	Stock @ cost plus VAT
Start-up		63,945	44,762	52,595
August	31,320	34,583	24,208	28,444
September	32,625	36,540	25,578	30,054
October	34,583	44,370	31,059	36,494
November	36,540	33,278	23,294	27,371
December	44,370	32,625	22,838	26,834
January	33,278	40,455	28,319	33,274
February	32,625	43,065	30,146	35,421
March	40,455	45,675	31,973	37,568
April	43,065	45,675	31,973	37,568
May	45,675	46,328	32,429	38,104
June	45,675	50,000	35,000	41,125
July	46,328	55,000	38,500	45,238
	466,538	571,538	400,076	470,090
Year 2				
August	50,000			
September	55,000			

Figures rounded to nearest pound

Fig. 7.12 OneShop's sales pattern and purchasing budget

Fig. 7.13 OneShop's cash flow forecast

	Aug	Sept	Oct	Nov	Dec	Jan	Feb	Mar	April	May	June	July	Totals:
Cash in													
Capital	70,000												70,000
VAT refunds				8,388									8,388
Cash sales	16,920	17,625	18,683	19,740	23,970	17,978	17,625	21,855	23,265	24,675	24,675	25,028	252,038
Credit sales		19,881	20,709	21,952	23,195	28,165	21,124	20,709	25,680	27,336	28,993	28,993	266,737
	86,920	37,506	39,392	50,079	47,165	46,142	38,749	42,564	48,945	52,011	53,668	54,021	597,162
Cash out													
VAT payments							4,880			1,961			6,841
Capital expenditure	4,700				1,175								5,875
Stock	52,595 / 28,444	30,054	36,494	27,371	26,834	33,274	—	35,421	37,568	37,568	38,104	41,125	424,852
Premises	5,875		5,875			5,875			5,875			5,875	29,375
Rates	100	100	100	100	100	100	100	100	100	100	100	100	1,200
Utilities				1,763			1,763			1,763			5,288
Insurance	2,000											2,000	4,000
Van lease	294	294	294	294	294	294	294	294	294	294	294	294	3,525
Petrol	196	196	196	196	196	196	196	196	196	196	196	196	2,350
Advertising	2,350				2,350				2,350				7,050
Legal start up	1,175												1,175
Legal/accounts	196	196	196	196	196	196	196	196	196	196	196	196	2,350
Drawings	3,000	3,000	3,000	3,000	3,000	3,000	3,000	3,000	3,000	3,000	3,000	3,000	36,000
Expenses	235	235	235	235	235	235	235	235	235	235	235	235	2,820
Total cash out	101,160	34,075	46,390	33,154	34,379	43,170	10,663	39,441	49,813	45,311	42,125	53,020	532,701
Monthly balance	(14,239)	3,431	(6,998)	16,926	12,785	2,973	28,085	3,123	(868)	6,700	11,543	1,000	64,461
Opening balance	0	(14,239)	(10,808)	(17,806)	(880)	11,905	14,878	42,963	46,086	45,218	51,918	63,461	
Closing balance	(14,239)	(10,808)	(17,806)	(880)	11,905	14,878	42,963	46,086	45,218	51,918	63,461	64,461	64,461

Quarterly VAT calculations

Input tax	Aug–Oct £	Nov–Jan £	Feb–Apr £	May–July £	Total £
Taxable sales	98,528	114,188	116,145	137,678	466,538
Total VAT payable on sales @ 17.5%	17,242	19,983	20,325	24,094	81,644
Output tax					
Stock	125,606	74,450	94,091	105,929	400,076
Capital expenditure	4,000	1,000			5,000
Premises	10,000	5,000	5,000	5,000	25,000
Utilities	1,500	1,500	1,500	1,500	6,000
Van lease	750	750	750	750	3,000
Petrol	500	500	500	500	2,000
Advertising	2,000	2,000	2,000		6,000
Legal/accounts	1,500	500	500	500	3,000
Expenses	600	600	600	600	2,400
Total purchases (VAT paid)	146,456	86,300	104,941	114,779	452,476
VAT element refundable @ 17.5%	25,630	15,103	18,365	20,086	79,183
VAT payable	(8,388)	4,880	1,961	4,007	2,461

Note: The business will receive a VAT refund in the first quarter as the VAT collected is less than the VAT paid on purchases.

Projected profit and loss account

	£	£
(Net of depreciation and finance charges)		
Sales		466,538
Purchases	400,076	
Less planned closing stock	73,500	
Cost of sales		326,576
Gross profit		139,961
Overheads		45,600
Net profit before taxes		94,361
Less drawings		36,000
Profit retained		58,361

Personal drawings

Susan has decided to draw £3,000 from the business each month to cover her personal needs.

Analysis of OneShop's completed cash flow forecast

■ For the first four months, OneShop will not have enough cash to meet its needs. This is because the initial capital injection of £70,000 is not sufficient to cover both capital and working capital requirements.

- An overdraft facility of £18,000 will be required, until the VAT refund on fixed assets and stock purchases is received in November.

- From November/December, monthly cash surpluses quickly turn the deficit into a healthy surplus.

- Predictably, the month's delay in paying for stock purchases from February gives a boost to OneShop's cumulative cash flow position (by reducing working capital requirements) from that date onwards.

- Fortunately, even if OneShop fails to secure one month's credit on stock the business will still maintain a cash surplus.

Where are OneShop's profits? (The balance sheet)

The relationship between OneShop's expected net profit of £94,361 and its cash in hand of £64,461 might not be readily obvious. You are probably curious to the whereabouts of two items – the original £70,000 capital and the £94,361 net profit (shown in the projected profit and loss account).

The answer is simply that some of the profits have been drawn out of the business by Susan and some have been retained and used, along with all of the original capital, to fund the purchase of fixed assets and working capital (ie investment in stock and debtors). Let's look at the picture in more detail.

Over the course of the year, Susan will have drawn £36,000 out of the business to cover her own personal living expenses and NI contributions leaving £58,361 in the business. Adding the retained profits to the original capital invested tells us the amount of capital that will be invested in the business at the end of the year – it is £128,361. As only £64,461 is left in cash, the rest must be in other assets.

Let's list them to find out if this is true. First the major assets (fixed assets) of the business.

	£
Fixtures and fittings	5,000

Next its current assets

	£
Cash on hand (from the cash flow)	64,461
The insurance and the first quarter rent has	7,000
been pre-paid (ex. VAT) – the VAT	
element has already been accounted for in	
the last quarter VAT calculation.	
Stock: two weeks' stock in hand to finance	73,500
August and September sales in year 2.	
Total from the purchasing budget (@ cost	
ex. VAT)	
Debtors – the actual sum owed (which	29,407
includes VAT)	
Total in current assets	174,368

However, OneShop has not had to find all this money. It has financed some of these current assets from outside sources. It owes money to a number of creditors. It is necessary to list and subtract all of these short-term liabilities from current assets to find out how much OneShop has had to use to fund its own working capital.

	£
Trade creditors (July stock purchase plus VAT):	45,238
the last delivery of stock has been invoiced,	
but no payment has been made.	
Utilities (last quarter used but paid).	1,763
VAT provision – the business owes Customs	4,007
and Excise a VAT payment for the last quarter	
of the year.	
Making total short-term (current) liabilities of:	51,007

Therefore, OneShop's working capital (net current assets) at the end of its first year trading is (current assets – current liabilities): £123,361.

If we now add the fixed assets to the net current assets, we will find the total amount of funds tied up in the business at the year end, £128,361, which is what was predicted. The total net assets have been financed by Susan's original £70,000 capital and the £58,361 profit retained in the business!

This completes a balance sheet of what Susan's business will look like at the end of its first year trading. If you take away all the detail, it is not that complicated. What remains is a list of where the business has obtained its money from (liabilities) and what it has done with it (assets) or, more simply, what it owes and what it has. The two lists are separated into long-term assets and liabilities, and short-term (current) assets and liabilities.

Exercise Try to answer the following questions about Susan's business. (You will find the answers in Figure 7.14, at the end of the chapter.)

Let's look at the worst possible position of OneShop; given the present sales and costs this would be:

- if debtors took two months instead of one month to pay up;
- if OneShop failed to secure one month's credit from suppliers of stock.

How much would this increase the working capital requirements by the end of the first year? Would the business be viable? If not, why not?

Note: You can answer the question by simply recalculating OneShop's working capital for the year end, but for a fuller picture, recalculate the cash flow forecast and draw up a new balance sheet. If you have access to the Internet you download a spreadsheet (in Excel format) to help you complete this exercise and to use in producing your own forecasts. (The support web site for *Starting Up* can be found from the main menu at http://www.ftmanagement.com.)

SUMMARY

You will need to calculate very carefully how much money you need to start and operate the business. The key to the successful management of your resources is the careful scrutiny and planning of your working capital requirements and cycle. A cash flow forecast is essential to any business. Never forget that cash is the life blood of any business.

A cash flow forecast is essential to any business.

Once forecasts have been made and budgets set, actual performance of the business should be closely monitored and any deviations investigated at once.

If your business idea has passed the tests of these last three chapters, you could have a potentially successful business. However, if it hasn't, don't despair, take it through the cycle again and see if it can be successfully modified. If the situation is worse than that, then you can be pleased that you never ventured any money on the enterprise and all that you have spent is time and effort. Try again!

 Checklist

1 What are your business needs?

2 Have you made a fixed asset requirements list?

3 Do you know the amount of capital each will require?

4 Have you considered the alternatives, such as buying second-hand, leasing, renting and so on?

5 Can you delay the purchase of some fixed assets?

6 Are they all really needed?

7 How much stock will you carry, on average?

8 How does this compare to other businesses of a similar type?

9 Can you arrange for more frequent deliveries?

10 Can you reduce your stockholding by any other methods?

11 What is the length of the working capital cycle?

12 Can it be reduced?

13 How much trade credit can you secure?

14 Can you obtain stock on consignment?

15 Can you organise your manufacturing process to reduce WIP?

16 How many days' credit will you give?

17 How many will you take?

18 Have you the necessary information on sales revenue, credit sales, costs and other outgoings to compile a cash flow forecast?

19 Have you produced a cash flow forecast?

20 Have you looked at the best and worst cash positions?

21 Have you relooked at your:

- working capital cycle
- fixed asset schedule
- reassessed your market for increasing cash sales
- overheads
- timing of costs
- to improve your cash position over time?

22 What proportion of your profits will have to be retained in the business at the year end to finance future expansion?

23 Other?

....

	Aug	Sept	Oct	Nov	Dec	Jan	Feb	Mar	April	May	June	July	Totals
Cash in													
Capital	70,000												70,000
VAT refunds				8,388									8,388
Cash sales	16,920	17,625	18,683	19,740	23,970	17,978	17,625	21,855	23,265	24,675	24,675	25,028	252,038
Credit sales			19,881	20,709	21,952	23,195	28,165	21,124	20,709	25,680	27,336	28,993	237,744
Total cash in	86,920	17,625	38,564	48,837	45,922	41,172	45,790	42,979	43,974	50,355	52,011	54,021	568,169
Cash out													
VAT payments	4,700						4,880			1,961			6,841
Capital expenditure	52,595												52,595
Stock	28,444	30,054	36,494	27,371	26,834	33,274	35,421	37,568	37,568	38,104	41,125	45,238	424,852
Premises	5,875		5,875			5,875			5,875			5,875	29,375
Rates	100	100	100	100	100	100	100	100	100	100	100	100	1,200
Utilities				1,763			1,763			1,763			5,288
Insurance	2,000											2,000	4,000
Van lease	294	294	294	294	294	294	294	294	294	294	294	294	3,525
Petrol	196	196	196	196	196	196	196	196	196	196	196	196	2,350
Advertising	2,350				2,350				2,350				7,050
Legal start-up	1,175												1,175
Legal/accounts	196	196	196	196	196	196	196	196	196	196	196	196	2,350
Drawings	3,000	3,000	3,000	3,000	3,000	3,000	3,000	3,000	3,000	3,000	3,000	3,000	36,000
Expenses	235	235	235	235	235	235	235	235	235	235	235	235	2,820
Total cash out	101,159	34,075	46,390	33,154	34,379	43,170	46,084	41,588	49,813	45,848	45,125	57,133	532,701
Monthly balance	(14,239)	(16,450)	(7,826)	15,683	11,542	(1,998)	(294)	1,390	(5,839)	4,507	6,866	(3,112)	35,468
Opening balance	0	(14,239)	(30,689)	(38,515)	(22,832)	(11,289)	(13,287)	(13,581)	(12,191)	(18,030)	(13,523)	(6,657)	
Closing balance	(14,239)	(30,689)	(38,515)	(22,832)	(11,289)	(13,287)	(13,581)	(12,191)	(18,030)	(13,523)	(6,657)	(9,769)	35,468

Fig. 7.14(a) Cash flow forecast – adjusted to show the effect of debtors taking two months to pay and the failure of the business to secure trade credit on stock purchases

	£	£
Fixed assets		
Fixtures and fittings		115,000
Total (A):		5,000
Current assets		
Prepaid bills (insurance and premises)	7,000	
Stock (@ cost ex. VAT)	73,500	
Debtors (July credit sales plus VAT)	58,400	
Total (B):	138,900	
Current liabilities		
Overdraft	9,769	
Utilities (last quarter used but paid)	1,763	
VAT provision	4,007	
Total (C):	15,539	
Working capital (B minus C)		123,361
Net assets employed in the business		128,361
Financed by		
Owner's capital introduced		70,000
Profits retained		58,361
		128,361

Fig. 7.14(b) OneShop's balance sheet at the end of its first year's trading – adjusted to show the effect of debtors taking two months to pay and the failure of the business to secure trade credit on stock purchases

Raising finance

How much is needed?

What will the finance be required for?

Sources and methods of finance • Grants

Reducing your need to borrow

Costs • Presenting your case • Summary

HOW MUCH IS NEEDED?

The first step, of course, is to establish the amount of capital required to start and operate the business. Chapter 7 should have enabled you to calculate how much will be needed and, perhaps more importantly, when it will be needed.

WHAT WILL THE FINANCE BE REQUIRED FOR?

The next step is to itemise what the finance is required for. This will set you on the right path to identifying the right kind of finance to secure. In the course of establishing your fixed and working capital requirements, you will, by implication, have identified the purposes for which they are required. Figure 8.1 indicates the appropriate methods of financing for particular purposes, while the next section deals with the methods and sources available in more detail.

Purpose	Method
Short-term finance	
Debtors, stock, raw materials and	Overdrafts
other general working capital	Creditors
requirements	Factoring
Long-term finance	
Fixed assets, longer-term	Loans (medium/long)
working capital requirements	Hire purchase
	Grants
	Mortgages
	Equity/venture capital

Fig. 8.1 Identifying the right kind of finance – a summary

SOURCES AND METHODS OF FINANCE

■ Short-term finance

The overdraft is perhaps the commonest and simplest form of finance available. You and your bank agree a limit to which you can overdraw on your account. You can then use part or all of that overdraft facility as and when you need it, which makes this form of finance very flexible. In addition, although the interest rate for over-drafts is usually a few percentage points above bank rate, the fact that you only take out the 'loan' when you need it can make it cheap to operate.

Overdrafts are ideal for covering such requirements as temporary cash flow problems. They should not, however, be used to purchase fixed assets or finance long-term working capital requirements. The reasons for this are that overdrafts have fluctuating interest rates and can be reduced or even called in by the bank at very short notice. This makes long-term financial planning with this method of finance extremely difficult. Moreover, it exposes the business to the real threat of insolvency.

Consider the situation below, where a business attempts to finance most of its working capital requirements with an overdraft facility:

Current assets	
Stock	£3,000
Debtors	£1,000
	£4000
Current liabilities	
Overdraft	£4,000

If the bank were to call in or reduce the overdraft, this might possibly force the business into bankruptcy, as the debtors and stock could not be easily or quickly turned into cash to repay the overdraft on demand.

To stand any chance of securing a business overdraft, the very least you must do is produce a fully justified cash flow forecast as described in Chapter 7.

■ Creditors

Securing trade credit from suppliers (as previously discussed in Chapter 7) is a good way of reducing your net working capital requirements and, therefore, your overall borrowing. The obvious advantage of this method is that it is interest-free. However, the problem is that suppliers are reluctant to grant such terms to new businesses. Possibly you will have to trade on a cash-on-delivery basis until you build up a good track record with your suppliers.

■ *Factoring*

For small businesses with a large proportion of their sales on credit, a major problem is finding the working capital to finance their customers' debt. If debtors do not pay on time, cash flow problems result. One way to alleviate the problem is a factoring service. A factoring service will advance up to 80 per cent of the value of credit sales as they are made, you receive the remainder when your customers settle their accounts. The cost of factoring varies from as little as 1 to 5 per cent of your sales turnover. The fee is affected by such considerations as the volume of sales involved, number and type of customers.

> *If debtors do not pay on time, cash flow problems result. One way to alleviate the problem is a factoring service.*

Besides easing cash flow problems, use of a factoring service can alleviate the problem of administration and control of debtors arising from credit sales. All you have to do is send the sales invoices to the factor who then takes over the whole process of collection.

Factoring is more suitable for businesses where sales are growing rapidly. By using the factor to finance debtors, cash flows into the business become predictable and, therefore, the expansion can be more easily managed.

Although there are many attractions in using a factoring service, it should be carefully compared with the advantages/disadvantages and cost of financing and administering your own credit sales. Because of the costs involved, businesses that have credit sales below £60,000 per annum seldom opt for this form of financing debtors. It should also be noted that using a factoring service reduces your personal contact with customers.

A list of factoring companies operating in the UK can be obtained from the Association of British Factors, 12th Floor, Moor House, London EC2Y 5HE.

▧ *Short-term loans*

These are obtainable from banks and finance houses, but have limited uses. They are less flexible than an overdraft and can work out considerably more expensive when the full amount is not used. However, they are usually easily arranged if the amount required is relatively small.

■ Medium- and long-term finance

▧ *Loans*

These are obtainable from banks and other financial institutions and are ideal for the purchase of fixed assets. Banks offer a variety of commercial loans repayable within one to ten years. Interest rates can be fixed or variable. You must shop around to see what is on offer. For instance, some packages contain repayment 'holidays' where you do not make your first repayment until some months after the loan has been advanced, giving your cash flow a boost in the early period of trading when it is perhaps most needed.

For the larger and longer-term capital loan, the lending organisation will probably require personal guarantees and security. Where the loan is a 'major' advance to be used to finance the main assets of the business, the lending institution will look carefully at the 'gearing of the business'. It will want to know how much you are putting into the business. For small businesses, banks may require you to put at least as much into the business as they are. Therefore, you will find it difficult to raise a loan in this way if you have less than a 50 per cent stake in your own business.

Note that many small businesses and SMEs prefer dealing with a bank, as the business relationship is more personal. If the bank is kept informed of the progress of your business, building mutual trust and respect, it is likely to be more sympathetic than other more impersonal lenders when problems occur.

▧ *Hire purchase*

Buying business equipment on hire purchase is just the same as buying household goods on hire purchase. The main advantage of using this method is that it is relatively easy to arrange and secure. The main disadvantages are that interest rates are usually considerably higher than for other forms of finance and any default on the loan may be pursued vigorously by the lender!

▣ *Mortgages*

This is a form of finance familiar to most people. Commercial and semi-commercial (when the mortgage is used to purchase a part-residential and part-commercial property) mortgages are advanced for the purchase of specific premises. The maximum loan advanced is usually up to 60 per cent of the valuation of the premises, but sometimes up to 90 per cent in the case of semi-commercial mortgages. Interest rates can either be fixed or variable and the period of the loan can be in excess of 20 years.

Note that building societies do not offer mortgages for industrial purposes. For this type of loan, you would have to approach such institutions as finance houses and insurance companies.

▣ *Equity finance*

This is, by definition, the most permanent form of finance, and is where an individual or organisation takes a share in your business. The main disadvantage is obvious – you can lose overall control of your business. The advantages are that there are no repayments involved and the launch of a business venture that you could not previously finance becomes possible.

Equity finance for new businesses goes under the name of 'venture' capital. As there are many sources and types of venture capital available, you should obtain specialist help. Details on venture capital organisations can be obtained from the British Venture Capital Association, 1 Surrey Street, London WC2N 2PS (Tel. 0171-286 5702).

GRANTS

I am sure everybody would love to start their business with 'free money'. There are many types of grants available from nearly as many different institutions and organisations, ranging from charities to local and central government bodies. It would take nearly the rest of this book just to go into the sources and types of funds involved.

The availability of grants and criteria for acceptance of applicants are dependent or based on some or all of the following factors.

- The area in which you intend to set up your business is an important factor. Most governments are keen to rejuvenate rundown localities, such as inner-city areas and underpopulated rural areas, particularly those that are suffering from a net migration of population.
- With a general increase in unemployment, your business is more likely to be eligible for a grant if it is going to create employment.
- Many grants and schemes are related to quite specific business activities. You would be well advised to try and identify the national/local private or public body/department representing your type of business activity and check on the availability of grants.
- Many governments are keen to promote the development of new businesses manufacturing, using and selling new technology.
- A number of grants and schemes are aimed at specific groups of the population – the disabled, 'socially disadvantaged', ethnic minorities, unemployed and so on.

REDUCING YOUR NEED TO BORROW

At the beginning of Chapter 7 you were encouraged to assess the financial needs of your business. Use this section to re-examine these – can they be reduced, redrafted or reorganised to reduce the amount you need to borrow?

■ Premises

Rent rather than buy? Renting can greatly reduce capital outlay, but, at the same time, it diminishes your capability to borrow further funds as little can be offered to the lender as security for the loan.

■ Equipment, machinery, fixtures and fittings and so on

Rent, lease or buy secondhand? The disadvantage of renting is that operating costs can be higher, but will this be offset by not having to pay charges and interest on loans to acquire the item that would otherwise have to be purchased. What are the benefits to be derived from releasing capital by this method for other purchases? Another factor to be considered is that rental and service agreements often offer service and maintenance. This helps you budget this aspect of operating costs more easily. If you are only going to use an item occasionally, can you hire it for short periods?

■ Stock

- Is your estimate for average stock level excessive?
- Can you adopt a different trading policy that involves a smaller range of goods to be carried without unduly harming sales potential?
- Can you obtain more frequent deliveries?
- Can you obtain stock on credit?
- Can you negotiate terms with suppliers where you only pay for the stock when you sell it (known as obtaining supplies on consignment)?

■ Debtors

- Can you increase your cash sales?
- Can you reduce the number of days' credit given to your customers?

COSTS

- Have you re-examined all of your costs?
- Can any be reduced?
- Can you use self-employed labour instead of employing staff?
- Can you link pay to sales?
- Can payment of your overheads be spread over a greater period of time?

■ Still can't raise enough?

If, after re-examination of the finance requirements, you still cannot raise the necessary capital, then don't despair. Calculate what scale of business the capital you can raise will support. A useful approach to this problem is to look again at the selling methods available to you. For instance, do you really need premises to sell from? Have you considered other methods of distribution (see Chapter 4)?

PRESENTING YOUR CASE

The main reason applications for business loans fail is that they are poorly researched and even more poorly presented. If you have researched and planned your business idea following the suggestions and techniques put forward in this book, you should not make this mistake.

The most important thing to remember is that the lender sees the loan in terms of their organisation making an investment in your business. They

The main reason applications for business loans fail is that they are poorly researched and even more poorly presented.

will, of course, want to know if their investment will be a profitable one for them. The key question in the forefront of their minds will be 'is there evidence of the ability to repay the loan?' With a person who is employed, this is relatively easy to assess by referring to the applicant's job (that is, how secure it is), salary and outgoings. With a business – particularly a new one without a proven track record – there is little solid evidence to prove the all-important ability to repay. This explains why a bank would rather lend £10,000 to an employed person with a relatively secure job to buy a car than lend the same amount to a person wishing to set up a new business. From the lender's point of view, one is relatively risk-free and the other fraught with risk. The lending organisation must therefore be convinced of your business' ability to repay them. The only way to do this is to prepare and present a business plan.

■ The business plan

The lender is likely to want satisfactory answers to the following, or similar, questions before granting the loan.

▓ *What is the business? Does it sound like a viable concern?*

The information required to answer these questions is as follows:

- A brief summary of the business idea.
- Basic information, including the business name, address, legal identity (such as sole trader, partnership, limited company – see Chapter 10).
- Information about the management of the business that is brief and concise, such as key personnel, their functions and so on.
- Details of the nature of your proposed business. What marks it out as being different from your competitors? Essentially, you need to project to the potential lender 'what business you are in' (see Chapter 2) and why your product and service will sell (see Chapters 3 and 4).

▓ *Are you the right type of person to run this type of business?*

The information required here includes a summary of:
- your personal details;
- relevant work experience, skills and education.

▓ *How much am I being asked to invest and for what?*

Here, the information required (see Chapter 7) is:
- the exact amount of money you want to borrow;
- how long you want to borrow it for;

- what exactly you are going to use it for – working capital, premises, fixtures and fittings and so on.

Does the business have a sufficient market for its product or service and will it be able to reach and exploit it?

To answer these questions, the following information is required (see Chapters 3 and 4 for more details):

- a summary of the market segments with particular reference to the revenue they are expected to generate;
- the market share expected;
- estimates of sales for each month in your first year;
- estimates of sales for the second year;
- details of how you will reach and sell to your markets;
- credible market research to back up all projections and statements.

Will the business make a viable profit?

Here, the following information is required (see Chapter 6):

- details of costs and sales, including timings;
- projection of when the business will be earning profits;
- breakeven analysis, showing the effect on the business of best and worst expectations;
- the expected return on capital employed.

Is the proposed business properly financed – does it have sufficient capital?

The information required here is as follows (see also Chapter 7).

- A projected balance sheet for the start of trading. This will show how the capital invested in the business will be used. It will also show the lender your intended equity in the business – that is, how much of the net assets employed in the business you are going to finance from personal funds. Most banks will expect you to have at least a 50 per cent holding in the business.
- A cash flow projection with explanatory notes. This is essential to show the lender your expected borrowing requirements over time. It demonstrates that the business will be able to remain solvent (that is, be able 'to pay its way'). The cash flow should include

repayments of the loan applied for – obviously essential as key evidence to the lending organisation that you will be able to repay the loan.

- Details of the working capital required and how it will be financed.
- Evidence that you have allowed for unforeseen costs and capital requirements.

■ *Other information*

In addition, you will have to include details of the security and personal guarantees offered in case the business fails. The actual way you lay out your loan application (business plan) is up to you to decide, but you must make sure you answer the potential lender's key concerns satisfactorily.

Many banks now produce their own guides as to how you should lay out your business loan application – they are usually in the form of a checklist of questions. The simple advice is to make sure you answer them!

When compiling your business plan, adhere to the following guidelines:

- Have it typed or word processed double-spaced with wide margins (this to allow the lender to make notes as they study it).
- The application should not be too long – try to go for a positive and concise presentation of the facts. Use diagrams and graphs where appropriate.
- Adopt a layout that makes sense and is easy to understand. Prepare the application in sections, number the paragraphs and pages so that you can easily refer the reader to relevant information, graphs and diagrams.

The complexity of the application will of course depend on the nature and scale of your business. If you find the task of compiling the report is beyond you, it is possible to pay for it to be produced. Obviously, you will still have to do the hard work of producing the information on which it is to be based.

Once completed, the application should be sent to or left at the lending organisation's offices a week before the interview to allow the lender time to study it. At the actual interview, quite naturally you will be nervous, but try and project an air of confidence (however, equally, don't 'go over the top'). Be positive, don't evade questions, be frank (lenders with experience are not easily fooled) and, above all, don't waffle. Dress smartly but conservatively for the occasion and, very important, watch your body posture. Many of us have very irritating habits that we are only partly aware of, such as continually tapping on desks, slumping in chairs, leaning too far forward when talking or looking anywhere but at a person when talking to them. Watch out for your bad habits. Remember, you have to sell yourself as well as your business.

> *The business plan is the crucial factor in any loan application.*

SUMMARY

Every business, at some time in its life, requires finance from external sources. You will need to know not just how much you need to borrow but also when. In choosing a finance package, it is important to consider the type of finance in relation to the specific use it will be put to.

The key questions any lender will ask are:

- **Is there the ability to repay?**
- **Is there adequate security?**
- **Does the applicant have sufficient equity in the business?**

The business plan is the crucial factor in any loan application.

The Internet and your business

1
2
3
4
5
6
7
8
9
10

INTRODUCTION

It is not that long ago that your choice of business location or selling medium would have been restricted to premises in the high street, a lease in an out-of-town retail park or some form of direct selling (see Chapter 4). However, the options open to small and large business to market and sell products and services has been significantly changed and widened by the recent phenomenal growth of the Internet and, more specifically, the World Wide Web. The continuing growth of Internet-based commerce will, with increasing numbers of consumers purchasing goods and services in virtual shopping malls, eventually affect most kinds of business, so you cannot afford to ignore or dismiss the Net.

You cannot afford to ignore or dismiss the Net.

This chapter gives you a basic understanding of what the Internet is, how it may affect your business and practical advice on how to establish an Internet presence that will meet the needs of your business.

Although the following serves as a good introduction to the Internet, it is the case that there is no substitute for being on-line and experiencing the Net first hand. You are strongly advised to gain some practical experience, which need not be expensive. There is certainly no need to go out and spend hundreds of pounds on a computer as many libraries now have Internet connections and you will find that your local further education college offers short courses on using the Internet.

THE INTERNET

Where else can you buy a book from the USA, check the weather forecast, send an electronic message to your friend and take part in a discussion about your favourite hobby without leaving your desk? Will the Internet be the biggest thing to happen to business in the new millennium? Nobody can yet answer that question, but certainly it is one of the biggest ideas of this century and no business can afford to ignore its continued dramatic growth.

It is really the advent, in 1992, of the World Wide Web and its now multimedia-rich pages and user-friendly features that has fuelled the growth of the Internet and attracted the interest of the business community. The World Wide Web is now used by businesses for such activities as advertising, customer support and direct selling.

Such has been the success of the World Wide Web that most people refer to it and the Internet interchangeably. The World Wide Web, however, is just one of the many services operating on the Internet. The Internet is really the infrastructure of the so-called 'information superhighway'. Indeed, you can liken it to a road network over which many different types of traffic flow.

The Internet (also referred to simply as the Net) is a collection of interconnected computer networks (an 'inter-network') spanning the globe, designed for the purpose of sharing information.

■ What is a network?

A 'network', explained at its simplest, is a number of computers (and other devices) that are connected together to enable them to share information and programs. The connections between the computers can be made in a number of ways, the most common being to use one of the many forms of network cable available, which plugs into a network card installed in each computer. This, however, is only the hardware side of the network – the part that provides the physical connection (known as the network media).

To enable one computer to 'talk' to another computer on a network a set of rules must be adopted to govern how data is transmitted across the connection media (the cables). This agreed set of communication rules is known as a 'protocol' – it is an agreement to converse in the same language.

The Internet makes use of a set of protocols known as TCP/IP (Transmission Control Protocol and Internet Protocol). It is the existence and adoption of TCP/IP that makes the Internet work and has allowed it to expand. To understand why this is so, it is necessary to take a brief look at the history of the TCP/IP and the beginnings of the Internet.

■ A very brief history of the Internet

Many people don't realise that the Internet started life in the 1960s, as a product of the Cold War. It was originally funded by the US military (the government agency was called the Defense Advanced Research Projects Agency – DAPRA) with the objective of building a communications network that would still function even if part of it were destroyed in a nuclear attack. This forerunner of today's Internet was called ARPANET and connected about 50 computers in military establishments and universities, mainly across the USA.

In the 1970s, research at Berkeley (University of California) led to the development of TCP/IP and, in the early 1980s, the US government mandated that all computers connected to ARPANET had to use TCP/IP. The year of the change to TCP/IP was 1983, which, coincidentally, was the same year Microsoft introduced the first version of Windows. ARPANET was split into two distinct networks:

- ARPANET became the civilian or academic network
- MILNET was created for use by the military.

The two networks were still connected, as the military had to communicate with academics working on military projects. IP (Internet protocol) was used to connect the two networks, routing messages between the networks, just as it does today on the Internet. Although IP, in those early days, only had to handle routing between two networks, it is the fact that it can handle routing of communications between literally thousands of networks that laid the foundations of the present-day Internet.

ARPANET's changeover to TCP/IP marked the birth of the Internet. The protocols can:

- operate on any kind of computer – which is why you can connect to the Internet regardless of the type of computer you own (although you are most likely to use a PC or Mac);
- connect together any number of different networks – which is why you can easily connect your local network (if you have one in your business) to the Internet and, if you do so, it can become part of the Internet (thus, the word 'Internet' really means the connection of networks);

- reroutes a message if one part of the network fails – which is why the Internet is resilient to network failures.

Another important factor that led to the early growth of the Internet was the decision by the US Government to make the TCP/IP specification freely available. This encouraged individuals and computer companies to develop programs for networks operating on TCP/IP, while at the same time preventing any company gaining a stranglehold on the technology, so TCP/IP is now an international standard. For this reason, TCP/IP is often referred to as the protocol of open systems.

■ How does it work?

To gain a basic understanding of how the Internet works, you can liken its operation to that of the telephone network. Every computer on the Internet – including the one on your desk, if you are connected to the Internet – has a unique number, just as your telephone does. This unique number is known as an 'IP address'. To connect to another computer on the Internet, your computer does the equivalent of what you do when you telephone someone. For example, if you wanted your computer to connect to the computer hosting the Financial Times Management web site, your computer would make a connection to the computer with the IP address 195.99.144.2. (all IP addresses take this form – four numbers separated by full stops.

An IP address shares other similarities with a telephone number in that part of it refers to the network address, just as part of your telephone number is the area code (STD). The remaining part of the IP address refers to the actual computer number ('host address') on the network, just as the right-hand part of your telephone number refers to your telephone on the local telephone network.

How any given IP address is divided between network and host is dependent on the 'class' of the address. At present, there are three classes of IP address:

Class A	Network	Host	....	....
Class B	Network	....	Host	....
Class C	Network	....	....	Host ....

For example, if the IP address 193.63.163.250 is a class C address, then the network address is 193.63.163 and the remaining number – 250 – refers to the actual computer on the network. If you apply for a block of IP addresses (you are unlikely to do so, for reasons given later), you would most likely be assigned a class C IP address block. This would give a total of 254 IP addresses to use on your local network – say from 193.63.163.1 to 193.63.163.254 (with 193.63.163.0 and 193.63.163.255 being reserved).

The Internet is a bit like a collection of towns (networks), each with a town gateway, connected by a system of roads.

You cannot exceed the number 255 because each part of the IP address is stored in a byte. Don't worry if you don't understand bits and bytes – they refer to the binary arithmetic the computer uses to perform calculations – all you need to know is that you cannot store a number greater than 255 in a byte!

As you can see the IP part of TCP/IP is responsible for addressing and moving data around the Internet. TCP is responsible for breaking up data into small chunks (known as 'packets') that the network can transport efficiently.

Put simply:

- TCP breaks the message to be sent over the network into packets;
- each packet contains the IP address of the destination network and host computer;
- if the packet is not for a computer on the local network, the packet is sent to a 'gateway' that knows about other networks;
- at the gateway, the packet is checked for the destination network address and is then routed (via other networks and gateways) to the destination network;
- when the packet arrives at the destination network, the host part of the address is read and the packet sent to the correct computer on the network;
- when the packets arrive at the destination computer, they are reassembled into the original message by TCP.

In more visual terms, the Internet is a bit like a collection of towns (networks), each with a town gateway, connected by a system of roads, some of these being narrow lanes, some motorways. The traffic consists of computer programs, text, pictures, video and sound moving between the towns. However, in this world of Internet towns and roads, there is no means of transporting information like a picture or a sound as a whole file. It must be broken up into parts and placed in containers known as packets before it can be moved on an Internet highway (or dirt track if no highway is available). In this cyber system of roads and towns, fortunately there is an intelligent traffic management system operated by 'routers'. These routers know about the amount of traffic on the roads and different routes to a town.

To flesh out our analogy a little further, let's assume a business in cyber town A wishes to send a picture to house 56 in town B. The TCP packer in the business breaks the picture into 20 packets. Inside each packet, the house number is written and on the outside of each packet the town letter. As the packets are not for the house in town A, they are sent to the town gateway for onward transit to town B. At the town gateway, the traffic system, managed by routers, decides the motorway is too busy and sends the first ten packets on a longer route to town B (sometimes using minor roads, occasionally passing through other towns). However, as the state of the roads can change quickly in cyber space, a lull in the traffic a microsecond later allows some of the remaining packets containing our picture to move down the motorway. When the packets arrive at town B, the town gateway examines the packets and finds the correct house address.

The packets containing all the parts of the picture eventually arrive at house 56 in town B, but because the packets were directed along different routes, the bottom half of the picture arrives before the top half. Fortunately house 56 also employs TCP, which knows how to reassemble the packets in the correct sequence. The picture is reassembled and the customer is happy.

THE WORLD WIDE WEB

The birth of the World Wide Web is attributed to Tim Berners Lee, a physicist at CERN in Switzerland. His idea was to develop a system that would allow non-technical network users to publish and view information easily. This he achieved based on a technology developed in the 1960s called hypertext.

■ The magic of hypertext

Hypertext is a simple but incredibly powerful technology. It enables one piece of information to be linked to another, no matter where it is stored on the Internet. One way to illustrate how this works is to use this book as an example. Assume you wanted to return to the section in this chapter entitled What is a network? If this book were on the World Wide Web, simply clicking on the words 'What is a network?' would take you to that page. To take the example a little further, assume I make a reference to the book in another book entitled *First Things First* by Patrick Forsyth. Clicking on the underlined text, 'First Things First', would present you with the first page of the book on your screen.

Figure 9.1 illustrates what happens when you use the World Wide Web. Let's say you start at a Web page found on a computer in the USA. A link on that page catches your attention and clicking on it takes you to a page on the same computer. That page contains a link to a Web page on a computer in Europe – clicking on the link will take you there. The page found on the European computer contains a link to information on a computer in South America. Again, you click on the link. Clicking on just three links has transported you across three continents.

■ Clients and servers

The illusion of the World Wide Web is such that you sometimes feel as if you are travelling from one place to another. However, in reality the information is coming to you, not the other way round.

Web pages are no more than a series of files stored on computers referred to as servers. These servers are sometimes no more powerful than or that much different to the computer sat on your office desk. The main difference is that they run web server software designed to respond to and deliver web pages to any computer on the Internet. The computer requesting a web page from a web server is

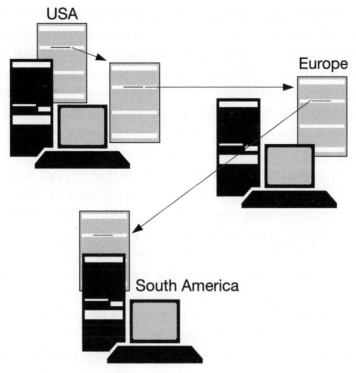

USA

Europe

South America

Fig. 9.1 Hypertext links

referred to as a client and uses software known as a 'web browser' to request and view the web page. Although there are many different vendors of browser software, the majority of people use either Netscape's or Microsoft's web browsers.

The exchange of information between the client (web browser) and server (web server) is managed via HTTP (Hypertext Transport Protocol). This explains why all web addresses (see next section) are preceded by *http://*. The protocol works with the TCP/IP to deliver web pages to your browser. There is no need for you to understand the technical details of HTTP, just that it exists and what it does.

Although web pages are just text files, they can contain links to other types of files, including images, video and sound. The layout of text, linking of images and other media into the pages is achieved using the mark-up language known as HTML (Hypertext Mark-up Language). As will be seen later, HTML is so easy to use that most people with very basic IT skills are perfectly capable of producing a simple web page.

The embedding of sound, images and video gives the World Wide Web its rich multimedia content. It is also possible to communicate with programs running on the web server, allowing, for example, users to search remote databases. This technology makes it possible for businesses to build web sites (collections of web pages and associated files) that allow customers to search catalogues, view images or short video clips of the product and even make purchases on-line.

The technology available to businesses and organisations that wish to publish on the World Wide Web is in constant development. For instance, the advent of a programming language called Java has enabled small programs called applets to be linked into web pages, giving the user a more interactive experience. Java applets are used to provide anything from conferencing to games.

For very little cost, anyone can rent space on a commercial web server operated by an Internet service provider (ISP) and publish a web page. This accessibility has led to the incredible growth of information found on the World Wide Web. Nobody knows for certain how many web pages there are, but it is certainly measured in millions.

■ Web sites have names

An organisation, business or individual will rarely publish just one page; rather they will publish a collection of interrelated pages. Such a collection of pages is known as a 'web site'.

In 1993, there were just a few more than 100 web sites on the World Wide Web, the number grew sixfold in the 6 months that followed and now the total number of web sites in existence is uncertain but it is numbered in millions.

Each web site has a unique name – a 'domain name'. For example, the FT Management web site's name is http://www.ftmanagement.com (note that the correct way of pronouncing a domain name is to use the word 'dot' every time a full stop is encountered). Notice that the domain name is divided into parts, separated by full stops, just like an IP address. This similarity is no coincidence. As will be seen later, domain names are 'mapped' against IP addresses.

Domain names represent a hierarchical naming system, which is controlled by an organisation known as InterNIC in the USA. The domain system is best understood if you read the domain name from right to left. The rightmost part of a domain name is the first level of the hierarchy, the next the second level (or subdomain) and so on finally ending in the host name of the computer. The format is:

Hostname • subdomain • second level domain • top-level domain

So, in the case of the FT Management web site, the web site resides on a computer called 'www' in the subdomain called 'ftmanagement' and is registered in the international first-level name space for company because its domain name ends in dot 'com' (see Figure 9.2).

First-level (or 'top-level') domains originally represented types of organisation, such as 'com' (company) – see Figure 9.3 for a breakdown of top-level domains by organisation type). As the Internet grew, it was decided that each country should have its own two-letter code. The UK's country code, not surprisingly, is 'uk'.

Name	Description
com	Commercial organisations
edu	Universities
gov	Government agencies
mil	US military sites
net	Internet service and infrastructure providers
org	Charities, miscellaneous and non-profit organisations

Fig. 9.2 Top-level domains by organisation

In the UK, NOMINET (http://www.nominet.net) is the naming authority responsible for managing second-level domains within the UK name space. These second-level domains are listed in Figure 9.3.

Name	Description
co.uk	Commercial enterprises
org.uk	Non-commercial organisations
net.uk	Internet service providers (ISPs)
ac.uk	Further and higher education
gov.uk	Local and central government
ltd.uk and plc.uk	Registered companies

Fig. 9.3 Second-level domains in the UK name space

■ Domain names and IP addresses

The whole purpose of domain names is to make life easier for Internet users. It would actually be possible to do without domain names and still be able to use the World Wide Web by using a web site's IP address instead of its domain name. If you have Internet access, try it for yourself.

Type the IP address 195.99.144.2 (in the open location dialogue of your web browser) you will reach www.ttmanagement.com. Obviously, it is much easier to remember than 195.99.144.2.

When you open a web site in your browser by typing its domain name, unseen, the web browser contacts a domain name server (DNS; by using its IP address) to 'resolve' (look up) the IP address for the web site. The domain name server then sends the IP address to your computer, which in turn uses it to locate the computer hosting the web site. Your computer uses the DNS system of servers just as you use a telephone book to look up a telephone number.

■ What is URL?

URL stands for 'uniform resource locator'. A URL gives the unique address for any given resource on the Internet, whether it is a web page, image, sound or some other file. A domain name on its own is a URL. Figure 9.4 explains each part of the URL.

http://	This stands for 'hypertext transfer protocol'. Other protocols are used on the Internet to manage the transfer of files, such as FTP ('file transfer protocol'), however HTTP is the most common.
www.ftmanagement.com	This is the domain name of the server on which the resource (usually a web page) can be found.
/catalogue	This refers to the directory (or folder) where the resource is stored. Directories can contain other directories (known as subdirectories), forming a tree-like structure starting from a root directory. Hence, URLs often contain many directory names making a 'path' to the file.
/Cathome.htm	This refers to the actual file to be fetched from the server. In this case it is a web page. All web page files have the suffix 'htm' or 'html' (hypertext mark-up language).

Fig. 9.4 The structure of a URL

E-MAIL

E-mail (electronic mail) pre-dates the World Wide Web and, for the majority of small businesses and SMEs, e-mail is the most often used Internet service. It is used for both internal communication, correspondence with suppliers and, not least, customer communications.

E-mail is not unlike ordinary mail in that you can send the equivalent of a memo or letter to anyone with an e-mail address. You can also include

> *E-mail (electronic mail) pre-dates the World Wide Web and, for the majority of small businesses and SMEs, e-mail is the most often used Internet service.*

with your e-mail any other type of file, so, for example, it is easy to 'attach':

- reports as a wordprocessed file;
- sales figures as a spreadsheet file;
- stock updates as a database file;
- sales presentation as a video file.

■ How does e-mail work?

E-mail is very similar to the postal system, with which we are all familiar. Assume you are sending a report with a covering letter to an organisation.

Ordinary post	E-mail
• You write a letter.	• You type your e-mail message on a computer.
• You attach a report.	• You attach the wordprocessed file that contains the report.
• You address the envelope.	• You type the e-mail address in the 'To:' section.
• You post the envelope.	• You press 'send' on your e-mail software.
• Your letter is sorted by your local post office.	• The e-mail is received by the mail server with which you have an account.
• It is received by the recipient's local post office	• The e-mail is received by the recipient's mail server, which places it in their 'mail box' awaiting collection.
• The local post office sends the letter to the recipient's house or business.	• The recipient uses a computer to connect to the mail server and collects their e-mail.

■ E-mail addresses

Like the postal system, e-mail works because every computer on the Internet has a unique address. An e-mail sent to you is actually sent to a computer operating as an e-mail server with which you have an e-mail account. The e-mail server holds any new mail for you until you collect it (using your computer and e-mail software). This is no different to mail being sent to your house and you collecting it from your letterbox.

An e-mail address is very much like your ordinary postal address. Most e-mail addresses look like this:

gary.jones@yourcompany.co.uk

The address is made up of two parts:

gary.jones	user ID, sometimes known as log in name, user name or account name – assigned by the network administrator (or Internet service provider – ISP) when you open your e-mail account;
@	*at*
yourcompany.co.uk	the Internet computer name/domain where you have an e-mail account.

■ The structure of an e-mail message

An e-mail message has a very similar structure to a business memo.

Field	Example	Meaning
To:	valued@acustomer.co.uk	The main recipient of the message
From:	sales@mybusiness.co.uk	The sender
Cc:	service@mybusiness.ac.uk	'Carbon copy' – copy sent to the customer service department of your business.
Reply to:	sales@another.address	If you want the reply to the message to be sent to a different e-mail address than the one you sent it from.
Attachment	readme.doc	Any file(s) you want to send with the message. In this case, the recipient will receive the file readme.doc

Dear Mr Jones
Your order has been despatched and you can expect delivery in the next 7 days.

'Message Body' – this is where you type your message. The message can be just a few lines or several paragraphs.

Attached is a revision to the design you agreed with our consultant.

For the latest additions to our product range visit us at ...

'Signature' – this is typed separately and stored so that it can be attached to the bottom of each message. The mail message can contain links to resources on the Internet. In this case, the signature used by the sales department is used to promote the product catalogue of the company's web site.

Sales Dept
My business
E-mail: sales@mybusiness.co.uk

■ The benefits of e-mail

One very persuasive reason for opening an Internet account is quite simply that over 50 per cent of small businesses and SMEs already have Internet connections and the number of UK domestic users exceeds 5 million. It can, therefore be argued that an Internet connection and e-mail account is second only in importance to having a telephone.

The success of e-mail in business is in little doubt, with the majority of business users regarding e-mail as essential. The benefits of e-mail to your business are many, not least that it is a fast and inexpensive way for customers to communicate directly with you and for you to respond quickly and efficiently to their enquiries.

The advantages of e-mail over other forms of communication include the following:

- a business e-mail account is inexpensive and is included as part of the service when you open an account with an ISP – the cost can be as little as £10 per month;
- you can send e-mail to anyone on the Internet for the price of a local call;

- messages (and attached files) arrive in minutes and, therefore, the time and cost savings can be enormous;

- messages containing confidential information can easily be encrypted (no technical knowledge is required);

- mailing lists can be used to send out mass mailings to customer groups at a fraction of the cost of a direct mail campaign using the postal service.

GETTING ON-LINE

To get connected to the Internet, you will have to buy an account from an ISP. An ISP is a business that resells Internet connectivity. The ISP maintains a network that is permanently connected to the Internet. This connection is sometimes via another provider, depending on the size of the ISP. Once you have an account with an ISP, you use your computer (equipped with a modem) to establish a connection to the ISP's network. For most small business users, an ordinary telephone connection (at local call rates) is sufficient.

Opening the account and setting up your computer to make the connection to the Internet is a fairly pain-free process. What is perhaps more difficult is to select an ISP that will meet your needs.

There is a growing number of ISPs. Some of the major ISPs – such as BT – have very large networks connected directly to the Internet that are capable of supporting many users. Others lease network connections from other providers. There is much talk about 'bandwidth', which means the amount

Speed of connection is obviously important, but there are other equally important criteria to consider. Availability, reliability and the types of services offered, not to mention cost, are some of the other factors you must consider when selecting an ISP.

of data that can be sent over the network connection per second. It is tempting to succumb to the argument that the bigger the ISP the bigger the bandwidth and therefore the better the Internet connection. However, the speed of your Internet connection will depend not just on the ISP's bandwidth, but also on the number of users sharing that bandwidth at any one time. The fastest way to get from A to B is the motorway, but not at rush hour!

Speed of connection is obviously important, but there are other equally important criteria to consider. Availability, reliability and the types of services offered, not to mention cost, are some of the other factors you must consider when selecting an ISP.

- **Cost** Most ISPs charge on a per month basis (typical charges at time of writing range from £10 to £25 per month). This is usually a flat fee for unlimited use of the Internet (of course, every time you connect you will pay the cost of a local call). Stay away from ISPs that charge by the hour.

- **Availability of connection** A good ISP will have sufficient telephone lines to ensure that you never experience an engaged tone.

- **Customer service** For most users, the quality and availability of telephone support to deal with technical questions is of great importance. Most ISPs provide helplines, but these should be checked for availability.

- **Services provided** Nearly all ISPs provide an e-mail account as standard and some web space to create a small web site. However, it is important to check that the web space provided can be used for commercial purposes. Many ISPs charge extra if you wish to publish a business web site. If you are interested in publishing a web site, you should also check the format of the URL the ISP will give you. Other URLs will be in the format of www.ispname.co.uk/~yourBusinessName. If you are planning a web site as a significant feature of your overall business strategy, you would be well advised to register your own domain name instead of using ISPs.

When selecting an ISP you would be well advised to purchase one of the many 'Internet magazines' that undertake monthly surveys of ISPs. Most magazines of this type carry free trial offers for some of the major ISPs. You can then try them and make your own judgement. Most of the free trials include web space, enabling you, if you wish, to try your hand at producing some simple web pages.

THE INTERNET MARKET AND TRENDS

Two of the most authorative sources of information about UK Internet usage and trends are the following.

- *Durlacher Quarterly Internet Report* (http://www.durlacher.com)
  These excellent reports, now sponsored by BT, are UK-focused.
  The key findings of each report are free and available either via
  Durlacher's or BT's web site
  (http://www.bt.com). Viewing of
  the full reports is restricted to sub-
  scribers. Each report focuses on a
  different aspect of the UK Internet market.

  > *The number of UK adults who have tried the Internet has increased by nearly 60 per cent.*

- **NOP's Internet user surveys** NOP conducts regular surveys of
  Internet usage in the UK. The key findings are published on their
  web site (http://www.nopres.co.uk) and are, again, essential to
  your market research if you are considering developing an on-line
  presence.

To access information on US/International Internet usage, visit the 'Interactive media' section of Nielsen Media Research (http://www.nielsenmedia.com/).

Available research suggests that there are in excess of five million Internet users (1998) in the UK. In the US, the figure is around 52 million (Nielson Media). More importantly, the number of users is growing at a dramatic rate. NOP reports that the number of UK adults who have tried the Internet has increased by nearly 60 per cent (12 months from December 1996 to December 1997) and the overall frequency of usage has increased to 5 times a week.

The number of web sites in the UK is also growing rapidly. The *Durlacher Quarterly Internet Report* (April 1997) reveals a 37 per cent growth in registrations in the 'co.uk' domain in the 3-month period from December 1996 to February 1997. Durlacher (in a survey conducted in March 1997) estimate that about 85 per cent of large UK companies have some form of Internet connection. Internet usage in SMEs is less, at 39 per cent, but an additional 20 per cent of SMEs indictated they would go on-line within the next year (*Durlacher/BT Quarterly Internet Report*, September 1997).

By the time you read this book, it is almost a certainty that the majority of UK businesses will be on-line, using e-mail for business communications, the World Wide Web to gather business information and establishing business web sites. Although surveys and their ensuing statistics and predictions should always be treated with caution, you should access on-line sources referenced in this section – they make interesting reading!

BUSINESS ON THE INTERNET

The information above should have eradicated any doubts you may have had about the continued growth of the Internet and its importance to business. Joining the on-line business community with a dial-up connection to the Internet is a relatively low-cost investment. It will allow you to share in the numerous benefits of being on-line, from researching competitors and finding suppliers to on-line marketing.

■ Marketing information

Chapter 3 covered in some detail the more traditional methods for researching marketing information. The advent of the World Wide Web, with its millions of web sites, has made it possible to access infinitely more marketing information than is offered by more traditional methods, often at no more cost than your Internet connection.

The principal means of searching for information on the Net is by using one of the many 'search engines'. Operated by companies such as Altavista, Yahoo!, Lycos and Excite, they offer you the ability to search the millions of web pages by key word or more complicated criteria. They are very easy to use and each carries help pages that, to make the most effective use of the service, you are well advised to study.

The search engines work by constantly crawling over the Internet, seeking out web sites, reading the contents and cataloguing the pages in very powerful databases. It is these databases that you remotely access every time you make a query via the search engine's web page. However, you should note, as no one owns or controls the Internet, no one search engine can hope to catalogue all the resources on the Net or be totally up to date.

■ *Using search engines*

- Always print-out and study the help pages for each search engine.
- Use the 'advanced search' facility (do not be put off by the word 'advanced') – it is easy to use.
- Remember that the search engine's database is not a complete listing of everything on the Net, nor is it always up to date. If you don't find what you want, try another search engine.
- Plan your information-finding sessions with care – this will result in saving time and finding higher-quality information. Remember that the search engine cannot 'read your mind'. Most search engines rank pages by seeking out your key words in catalogued web page titles and then counting the frequency of your key word in the page. This works well most of the time, but can result in URLs to web pages that are totally irrelevant. For instance, using the Net to locate competitors retailing mobile phones may prompt you to enter 'mobile phone' and 'supplier'. As a result you may get pages containing a list of mobile phone numbers for employees or pages that appear in your returned listing because they include somebody's mobile telephone number who is a supplier of some other service or product.

In addition to search engines, there are various business directories on the Internet. Of particular interest to UK small businesses are the following (the site details are correct at the time of researching for this publication, but you should be aware that URLs and the services offered by these companies might change).

- **Electronic *Yellow Pages*** (http://www.eyp.co.uk) A web version of British Telecom's *Yellow Pages* directory, listing contact details of over 1.5 million UK businesses. Searchable by location or category and company name.
- **Thomson Directories** (http://www.inbusiness.co.uk) You can search over 2 million UK businesses by company name and location. Also, you can add your business to their database.
- **Kelly's** On-line database of 12,000 UK companies. Also contains links to major newspapers, chambers of commerce and Business Link web sites.

- **Dun and Bradstreet** (http://www.dbeuro.com/UK/uk_home1.htm) After registration (which was free at the time of my last visit to this site) you can search for businesses by type of business, turnover and number of employees, from a database of 2 million businesses.

- **British Exports Interactive** (http://www.britishexports.reedinfo. co.uk/) A site devoted to developing international trade between UK exporters and overseas companies.

- **Martex** (http://www.martex.co.uk) Provides a listing of a number of trade associations in the UK and, in turn, listings of members and links to their web sites.

- **Yahoo! UK** (http://www.yahoo.co.uk/Business_and_Economy/) An excellent place to start when wishing to explore business sectors in the UK.

This represents only a small fraction of the information available to your business. In addition, you will find that all major newspapers and many journals have web sites. Most market research companies are also to be found on the World Wide Web, but, unfortunately, their services do not come free.

> To generate traffic to your web site, you can also take advantage of something called 'banner advertising'.

■ Advertising

The great thing about the World Wide Web is it is open 24 hours a day, 365 days a year, used by millions of people and publishing information on it is both relatively easy and cheap. Sounds like the perfect place to advertise? Unfortunately, there are two major drawbacks that the less reputable web design and hosting companies may fail to tell you about:

- with well over a million web sites, your advertising message could be like a message in bottle thrown into the Atlantic ocean – your beautifully designed web site may attract only a handful of visitors;

- as the World Wide Web is fast becoming a mass market, the problem, increasingly, is a matter of how to target your advertising effectively.

Both problems can be overcome, however, providing that your web site has been subject to careful planning and professional design from the outset. The majority of Net users access search engines and directories to locate web sites, so all that needs to be done is to register your site (there is no charge) with the major search engines and directories. In doing this, the problem of targeting your site is, by default, partly solved. Users entering key words associated with your business may have links to your site returned by the search engine. However, whether or not your business will appear in the top ten links returned to the user cannot be guaranteed. This is partly dependent on the skill of the person who coded your web pages and their understanding of how each of the major search engines work (although this is outside the scope of this introductory chapter, you can find out how each search engine catalogues and ranks web pages by visiting their site and following the link that is usually marked 'add URL').

To generate traffic to your web site, you can also take advantage of something called 'banner advertising'. This is the World Wide Web's equivalent of taking advertising space in a newspaper or the *Yellow Pages*. You create an advert graphic and pay to have it placed on a web site that has a visitor profile that matches your target market. When the user clicks on the banner, they are taken to your web site. You usually pay an initial fee for the design of the banner (you could cut costs and design it yourself) and its placement. In addition, you pay according to either the number of times it has been displayed or number of 'clicks' (the times a user has clicked and used the banner to access your site).

You can also buy advertising banner space on web search engines or directory sites. Then, you pay to have your banner advertisement displayed when the user of the search engine enters selected key words. In this way, you can finely target your advertising. The major drawback of this approach, when using some of the larger search engines and 'buying into' more popular key words, can be the cost (check out the search engine sites for the current rates).

A lower-cost approach to building traffic on a web site is to sign up to a free banner exchange scheme. The principle is simple enough – you agree to host advertisement banners served from your chosen banner exchange scheme and, in return, your banner is shown in rotation on participating scheme members' web sites. It acts like a cooperative. All you need to do is agree to the rules of the scheme and provide a graphic of the required size. You can usually specify the types of sites you wish your banner to appear on, thus fine-tuning the targeting of your web site and advertising. At the time of writing, two of the more popular exchange schemes are:

- Link Exchange (http://www.linkexchange.com);
- Banner Swap (http://www.bannerswap.com).

Perhaps one of the greatest advantages the Web has over other forms of advertising media is its ability to provide interactivity with the customer. As has already been seen, users of the World Wide Web can be targeted and reached. The objective is then to get them to communicate with your business. On the Net this is more easily achieved than is the case with other forms of advertising media. The potential customer, in response to your web advertisement, can use e-mail or fill in electronic forms to make direct contact. They can also be encouraged to search for and view products and even shop on-line. Further, you can ascertain the effectiveness of your web site in achieving its objectives from logs kept by the web server. These logs can furnish you with information ranging from the number of visitors in a given period to how they behaved on their visit. It is also possible to 'script' a web site so that it recognises a repeat visitor and personalises their visit.

■ On-line shopping

The market for electronic commerce is huge – some estimates valuing worldwide transactions for 1997/8 at over 2 billion US dollars, with a predicted rise to over 20 billion US dollars by 2001. Even if such estimates prove to be vastly optimistic, there is little doubt that the Internet is set to become a huge marketplace. What's more, it is a marketplace, in theory, that even the smallest business can enter.

The on-line shopping process is quite simple. Assuming a customer has viewed your product or service on-line and wishes to buy, they click a link to a 'secure' section of the web site to make the purchase. 'Secure', in this context, meaning the details entered by the customer are encrypted before they are transmitted to the web server. The business then accesses the details, again using an encrypted channel. The process is then no different to a telesales operation.

There are no barriers to setting up on-line shopping in terms of either the technology or the cost and, indeed, most ISPs providing commercial web space now offer secure web space at no extra cost. The main problem is convincing your bank to allow you to take credit card transactions in this way. At the time of researching this book, it would appear there is a growing trend for banks to develop there own net services or forming associations with a limited number of ISPs. Therefore, your choice of ISP may be limited to those authorised by the banks. Some ISPs that I contacted have schemes where you use one of their merchant services' accounts and leave the processing of the credit card transaction to them. This obviously has benefits in terms of reducing the administration, but the downside is they take a percentage cut of the sale and you usually have to wait 30 days for payment. It is to be hoped that attitudes will change before too long as the transmission of information over the Internet (using encryption) is far more secure than giving credit card details over the telephone.

Given the current attitudes of banks to Internet transactions, you may be well be forced to use more traditional forms of response to handle on-line sales. Your web site can handle the first part of the sale – generating the interest and desire for your product, even providing the customer with a virtual shopping trolley. At the point at which you would close the on-line sale, the customer can view or print out their order and then pay by telephone, fax or post. The experience of many businesses is that this mix of technologies works well. Even if you can convince your bank to allow you to take credit card payments on-line, you would be well advised to allow customers to use alternative ways to pay.

If your business sells only to account customers, you may well consider that accepting orders via a web site or e-mail is more efficient and provides improved customer service. A system such as this is, again, relatively easy to set up by making an area of your web site accessible only by account number and password. Once your account customer has gained access to this secure area of the web site, they can complete their order using a fill-in electronic form.

BUSINESS WEB SITES

Earlier in this chapter, the uses and benefits of an on-line presence for your business were discussed in some detail. If you decide to establish your business on the World Wide Web, the information and guidelines in this section will help you to do so. However, in the space available, the information given here can only serve as an introduction to some of the many issues related to establishing a business web site and so you should explore all aspects further to see how your particular business is affected.

■ Domain names

A potential customer will access your web site either by following a link returned by a search engine or typing the URL of the site. The format of your web site's URL is of major importance for this reason and also because you should include it in all business stationery and advertising media. Essentially, there are two choices open to you for selecting a URL for your web site:

- either accept the one offered to you by your ISP;
- or register your domain name.

Of the two options, registering a domain name is by far the better option as:

- a domain name represents a shorter and more easily remembered web address;
- a domain name can be selected to associate with a brand or trading name;
- your web site will always be associated with your domain name, even if you move your web site to another ISP (this is perhaps the most important reason for registering a domain name);
- your e-mail address will also include your domain name, helping

to convey a consistent on-line image, so, again, your e-mail addresses will stay with you as long as the domain name is registered;

- registering your domain name prevents others from registering your trading name as a domain name. At present domain names are issued on a first come first served basis.

The process of registering a domain name is normally handled by the ISP you select to host your web site. At the time of researching this book, typical costs for registering a domain name in the '.co.uk' format were £50 set-up costs (ISP administration charge), £60 administration costs for 2 years and £30 per year for subsequent years (payable to the naming authority).

You should take care that the domain name you select is not already in use as a trading name by some other company. This can be checked by employing the services of a business names registry for a fee of approximately £50 (some ISPs also offer this service).

■ Designing a web site

The subject of web site design is worthy of a full book in its own right. However, for the sake of brevity here, let us look at the main points.

In its broadest sense, this topic covers the development of your on-line strategy (purpose/objectives of your web site), including strategies for building traffic and repeat visits through to site navigation/structure and the nitty gritty of web page design and coding.

■ Deciding what you want to achieve

- **To establish a presence** You may wish to simply establish a presence on the Internet. Many businesses on the World Wide Web are there simply because competitors are on-line. The problem with this motivation is that there is a very real danger of establishing a web site that is no more than an electronic business card. Worse, if it is badly designed, it will do more harm than good to your business' image. If you have not clearly defined the purpose of your site, then what will the reaction of an on-line visitor be? You are better building a presence by focusing on and promoting an aspect of the company or one of its products.

- **To promote a product or service** As discussed earlier, a web site with this focus, if it is professionally designed and promoted, can be integrated into an advertising campaign. Your site should drive towards obtaining visitor feedback via use of on-line fill-in forms, e-mail, telephone, fax or traditional mail. Further, you may consider offering incentives, such as product discounts for visitors who register their details while on-line. This will allow you to measure the response and build up a valuable mailing list to aid direct marketing.

- **To improve customer service** If your customers are users of the Internet, then a web site can be focused on providing customers with information, dealing with technical queries, responding to enquiries regarding delivery dates and so on. Using a web site for this purpose can represent a considerable saving over, say, using telephone support. Although all web sites require trained staff to update and respond to e-mail enquiries, be prepared to invest more in support for this kind of site.

- **To provide publicity, improve public relations** If your type of business warrants it, then a web site can be used to issue press announcements. To develop the business image in the desired direction, you could consider sponsoring a charity or similar organisation and associating your business name or brand with the site. The web site would focus, first, on the sponsored organisation and, second, on your brand. Obviously, for business benefits to ensue, the association of the brand with the charity must be a positive one. A similar approach is to build a web site that focuses on your targeted customer's hobby rather than the product. For example, if you are in the business of producing cat flaps (not the most interesting product in the world), then you will build more traffic and interest in your products by developing a web site for cat owners where they can obtain information free of charge about such things as cat health, breed information and so on.

- **To open up international markets** With a web site, you can open up a dialogue with international markets as easily as with a prospective customer in the next town. Before the advent of the World Wide Web, such opportunities may well have been closed to you on the basis of cost alone.

■ **To sell on-line** This is the aim of most businesses wishing to develop an on-line strategy. It is one that has been discussed earlier and, although there are some inhibitors, there is no reason for it not being part of your overall Internet strategy. I would advise that you too start small and attempt to encourage direct customer response to on-line advertising using the methods outlined above.

This represents just some of the uses of a business web site. Whatever your general aims, it is essential you are able to provide answers to the following questions.

■ What are your plans to promote your web site, both on-line and in traditional media?

■ When a customer reaches your home page, what will hold their attention long enough so you can convince them to proceed further?

■ What do you want a customer to do once they have reached the home page of your site?

■ What is the most appropriate site content to spark customer interest?

■ What frequent updates to the site can you make to ensure repeat visits?

Having refined your ideas for the web site, the next decision is whether or not the production of the web site should be handled in-house or contracted out. The decision will be partly based on whether or not you have staff with appropriate skills. This said, as we have seen, even those with only fairly basic IT skills can produce a web page. Web pages are just text files, which can be produced by anyone who can type. They contain codes in the form of tags (key words surrounded by brackets). This code is known as HTML (hypertext mark-up language). Some mistake it as a computer programming language, which it is not, and wrongly assume it is difficult to learn. However, HTML can be mastered by anyone who can operate a computer and has a basic understanding of file names and directory structures.

The problem with in-house development of web pages is the time it may take to develop your skills in HTML and other web technologies (not to mention graphics and the basics of graphic design). Before you rush to your local bookseller to buy the latest book on HTML, you should consider whether your own or your staff's time is better spent managing other aspects of your business.

There are many software packages available that automate many aspects of site design (using templates and wizards). Many also claim that you do not need to understand any HTML to create pages. While the claims are, in the main, justified, things do go wrong, and a basic understanding of HTML and how the Web works is essential. If you are prepared to invest in suitable software and spend some time learning the art of web design, there is no reason to assume that you cannot design and produce your own site.

■ Choosing a web site designer

Considering the time and effort that must be spent to build up the level of skill required to produce an effective web site, it may be appropriate to contract the services of a professional web designer. This, however, does not remove the need for the analysis suggested in the previous section – you will still have to identify the objectives for the site and provide the text content. You can expect the web designer to advise you on the content, how to promote the site, build into the design easy updating and, of course, design the structure, pages and graphics. The cost can vary considerably – depending on the complexity of the site required – ranging from a few hundred to tens of thousands of pounds.

Before you select a web designer, ensure that you have done the following:

- familiarised yourself with the Internet – if you have read and understood this chapter, you should be ready;
- gained experience on-line – either by attending an introductory short course at college or via your own Internet connection;

- completed a survey of your competitor's web sites (you may wish to use the competitor profiling sheets given in Chapter 3);
- clearly identified the objectives of the web site;
- decided on some criteria to measure the success of the web site (such as the number of visitors or customers' e-mail responses);
- outlined the text content of the proposed web site;
- selected possible images for use in the web site.

To help you select a web designer, use the following checklist:

- the web designer should have their own web site – evaluate it;
- ask for a list of clients (these should be linked to the designer's web site) – evaluate their sites;
  - can you clearly identify the site's purpose?
  - does the site hold the visitor's attention/interest?
  - is it easy to navigate the site?
  - can the site be found easily using the search engines?
- use at least two different browsers (such as Netscape and Internet Explorer) and screen resolutions to evaluate all sites produced by the designer;
- ask for references;
- check to see if the designer has produced sites similar to your intended site;
- see if the designer can build the site in such a way that it can be updated by your staff without a large investment in training;
- does the designer retain copyright over the images, coding and other non-textual components of the site?

■ Selecting an ISP to host your site

There are several options for hosting your site. The very low-cost option is to use the free web space that comes with an Internet dial-up account. This is fine for 'DIY prototypes' and to cut your teeth on the technology. However, if you have spent time or money developing a professional web site, then you should lease commercial web space from a suitable ISP. The principal benefit of commercial web space is faster access. The third option is to buy your own server and rent space on an ISP's network. This gives you the ultimate in control and is essential if you wish your web site to, say, link to a booking system or some other database. This kind of control comes with a starting price of around £2500 per year plus the cost of equipment, software and a member of staff to maintain the server and site.

For most small businesses and SMEs, leasing commercial web space is the best option. The cost is around £25 per month per 10 Meg of disk space (this is ample for a business web site.

The following is a basic checklist to use when selecting a provider of commercial web space.

 Checklist

1 What kind of technical support is provided? A good ISP will provide customer support via the telephone, e-mail and have a section of its own web site devoted to providing information on how to get the best from your commercial web space.

2 Does the ISP provide secure web server space at no extra charge?

3 Is there a guarantee regarding the availability of the web server on which your site is hosted – what happens if the server goes down?

4 Check the ISP's web site – it should have links to the business web sites it hosts. Evaluate the speed of the connection to these sites at different times of the day.

5 Ask the ISP if it can provide testimonials from present clients.

6 Check the small print – under what circumstances can the ISP terminate the contract or take your site down?

7 Is there a traffic limit (in Mbs or hits per day) on your web site? If so, what happens if you exceed that limit? A good ISP should make its policy on this clear and detail the charges for additional traffic over the limit. A bad ISP will take your site off-line if you exceed the limit (sometimes without telling you).

8 Does the ISP provide domain registration services? Is it included in the price? If not, carefully check the full price of setting up and administration of the domain (including fees payable to naming authorities)? Also check these prices against other ISPs (some bad ISPs have been known to vastly inflate their fees for this service). Also, check that you can use your domain name for e-mail and how the e-mail accounts are set up.

9 All ISPs providing commercial web space should provide server logs to allow to you to analyse your web traffic. Ask how you access the logs and what details they provide.

10 Ask the ISP if it allows you to run CGI scripts. CGI scripts are small programs that run on the server in response to requests from a client web page from your site. CGI programs are useful for implementing such web site features as forms designed to capture customer details and other interactive features. CGI programs represent a security risk for ISPs, but this problem can be solved by running a CGI program in a 'wrapper' (another program that prevents the CGI program accessing other files and systems outside your web space). A good ISP will allow you to run CGI programs, but require you to submit them first for checking.

11 If you wish to use your web site to complete on-line credit card transactions, you will need to check whether or not the ISP has been approved by the bank with which you hold a merchant services account.

SUMMARY

The Internet is the infrastructure of the information super highway on which a range of services is available. Of principal interest to businesses are e-mail and the World Wide Web.

E-mail is nearly as important to a business as the telephone. Over 5 million consumers and the majority of businesses in the UK have access to e-mail. E-mail is both faster and cheaper than postal mail and is excellent for interbusiness communication and direct marketing.

The World Wide Web is a vast source of information for businesses and can be used for such activities as evaluating competitor activity. The cost of a business web site is within the reach of the smallest business. Web sites can be used for a range of activities, from advertising and customer service to on-line commerce.

On-line commerce is still in its infancy in the UK, but all predictions indicate huge growth as Internet usage continues to expand and the technology becomes cheaper and more accessible. Small businesses and SMEs considering on-line commerce chould consider starting in a simple way by initiating the sale on-line, but completing the transaction using more traditional methods. It is wise to consult fully with your bank if you are planning to develop a web site to take on-line credit card transactions.

To establish a successful web presence, you must have a basic understanding of how the Internet functions. To be successful online requires the same attention to detail and careful planning that is associated with any other business activity. Be prepared to invest time in planning the purpose and content of your proposed web site before contracting a web site designer. Also, it is recommended that you register a domain name for your web site and e-mail.

Your Internet presence should reflect your business identity and be integrated into your overall marketing strategy.

Before you start up, have you ...?

1
2
3
4
5
6
7
8
9
10

INTRODUCTION

If you have used each chapter in this book to help you research and plan your business venture, you will now be nearly ready to 'start up'. However,

You should also take one last look at your business venture before you start up.

there are still some important considerations left, such as the legal form your business should take, tax considerations and licences. You should also take one last look at your business venture before you start up. This is the purpose of this chapter, to tie up loose ends and provide you with a general checklist before you take the final step.

THE LEGAL FORM OF YOUR BUSINESS

Legally, all businesses fall into one of the following main categories:

- sole trader
- partnership
- limited company
- cooperative

Each of these has its own advantages and disadvantages. Your choice depends on weighing up the pros and cons in relation to your business needs

Setting up as a sole trader is perhaps the simplest way of entering into business.

– and there is no right answer. Your accountant and solicitor should be able to advise and help you come to a decision. What follows is a brief description of each form and a summary of their main advantages and disadvantages.

■ Sole trader

Setting up as a sole trader is perhaps the simplest way of entering into business. From a legal point of view, there is nothing you have to do to set up in business as a sole trader.

Advantages
- Easy to set up – there are no legal formalities.
- You have total control of the business.

- You are taxed as an individual.
- Accounts do not have to be disclosed to the public.
- Easy to wind up.
- Some tax advantages in the short term.

Disadvantages

- You are totally responsible and liable for all business losses. If the business goes bankrupt, so do you. Your creditors will be entitled (through the courts) to seize your personal as well as business possessions.
- Does not have the status of, say, a limited company.

■ Partnership

If two or more people go into business together without registering as a limited company or cooperative, they are forming a partnership. Again, you can enter into business like this without any legal formalities. However, you would be ill-advised to enter into a partnership without a formal partnership agreement, even more so if you are entering with a relative or close friend. The main reasons for this are to prevent severe disagreements about how the business should be operated and, should the partnership be wound up or sold, how the proceeds should be distributed. Remember, all may seem rosy now, but the best of

You would be ill-advised to enter into a partnership without a formal partnership agreement.

friendships do not always last for ever, particularly when exposed to the stresses and strains of running a business. The partnership agreement is there to protect you, your friendship and the business.

Partnership agreements should cover the following as applicable.

- Who is responsible for what?
- How many hours should each partner devote to the business?
- When and for how long can each partner take their holidays?
- How much can each partner draw out of the business?
- Will cheques to be drawn on the business' bank account require more than one partner's signature?
- How are major decisions to be reached? One vote per partner or otherwise?

- Will there be any system for settling disputes between partners?
- How are the profits to be divided?
- How long should the partnership last?
- How much notice should be given if one partner wants to withdraw?
- How will the proceeds of the business be split up if the partnership is dissolved?
- Will there be a provision for accepting new partners into the business?
- What happens if one partner dies? Will the partnership be automatically dissolved?

The list could be almost endless. There are obviously all kinds of eventualities to be considered. Some partnership agreements, because of the nature of the business, are simple; others more complicated. What should be in your partnership agreement? Sit down with your partner(s) and work out the rough details, then go to see your solicitor for further advice.

Advantages

- A good way of pooling complementary skills and knowledge.
- A way of starting a business that requires more capital than you have at your disposal.
- Can help share the workload and pressures associated with running a small business.
- Other advantages similar to those of being a sole trader, except you are not totally responsible.

Disadvantages

- Each partner is responsible for all business debts, even if incurred by another partner.
- There are some legal costs involved in drawing up a partnership agreement.
- There is always a risk of personality clashes ruining the business.
- The death or bankruptcy of any one partner, unless there are arrangements to the contrary, will automatically dissolve the partnership.
- Can be difficult to expand the business by introducing new partners.

■ Limited company

The word 'limited' in this context means your liability to repay the business debts is 'limited' to the amount you have agreed to contribute to them. Therefore, if the business goes bankrupt, your personal possessions cannot be seized to pay the company's debts. This is, as you can imagine, the greatest attraction of forming a business in this way. However, there are a number of disadvantages (see later). A limited company has a legal identity that is separate from its shareholders. Like an individual, the company itself can enter into contracts with other organisations and individuals, sue and be sued and prosecuted without involving its shareholders in the proceedings. Put simply, once a limited company is formed, it exists in its own right and will remain in existence indefinitely, even if it ceases trading, until such time as action is taken to wind it up.

A limited company is formed with a minimum of two shareholders. A director must be appointed from the shareholders, and a company secretary appointed, who can be an outsider. With a small business, this is usually the business' accountant or solicitor. Further to this, a limited company prior, to registration, must produce, and later adhere to, two principal documents – the memorandum and articles of association. These are complicated documents but can be simply summarised as follows.

The memorandum sets out the main objectives of the company. These are usually set quite wide to allow the company to sell or manufacture other products and services as it expands. The memorandum details the company's share capital. The articles of association set out additional rules by which the company will be governed. In many ways, it is similar in content, but not style, to some aspects of a partnership agreement. To the lay person, both documents can be incomprehensible as they tend to overuse legal jargon. However, most use standard phrases and, therefore, you will find that many memorandums and articles of association are similar. As you can see, specialist advice from a solicitor is needed if you wish to form or 'buy' a limited company.

If you wish to have limited company status, there are two options open to you. You can buy one 'off the shelf' or start one from scratch. Buying one 'off the shelf' means buying an existing company that has no assets and is not trading. These 'off the shelf' companies are offered for sale in the UK by specialist companies known as 'company registration agents'. They keep a stock of companies (that they have properly registered) suitable for a range of businesses. On 'transfer' of the company to its 'new owners', all that has to be done is for the existing shareholders (nominees of the company registration agent) to resign to allow the purchasers to become the new shareholders and appoint directors. Because there is less legal work to be done in buying a ready-made company, it is the cheapest method. However, the way you intend to establish your business may demand that you start a company from scratch. If this is the case, expensive legal work can increase the costs from hundreds to thousands of pounds.

If you wish to have limited company status, there are two options open to you. You can buy one 'off the shelf' or start one from scratch.

If you form a limited company, you, as one of the directors, will have the following responsibilities:

- you will have to attend properly conducted Board meetings;
- you will have to disclose interests and shares in the company;
- you must take reasonable steps to make sure you know what is going on in your company and act in a manner that is honest and diligent;
- accordingly, if you allow the company to trade while knowing it can't meet its debts, you may well find yourself personally liable;
- you may not borrow money from the company;
- you cannot exceed the powers granted to you in the articles of association;
- you must be elected by the shareholders and, accordingly, you can be removed by them.

Advantages

- Limited liability.
- Higher level of status/improved image.
- Capital may be increased by selling shares.
- You will be an employee of the company.
- Management structure of the business is better defined.

- The business is not affected if shareholders die or become bankrupt.
- Disposal or acquisition of shares can easily be arranged.

Disadvantages

- Limited liability status can, to all intents and purposes, be removed by the increasing practice of lending institutions asking for personal guarantees from directors and major shareholders.
- Can be very costly to set up.
- The business will have to make public its accounts, which means telling your competitors what your sales, costs, assets, liabilities were last year!
- You will probably need continuing professional advice to meet your legal obligations as a limited company.
- As an employee of the company, you will be subject to PAYE.
- You can only start trading after the company has been properly formed.

■ Cooperative

Forming a cooperative is only suitable for those people setting up in business with a strong wish to adhere to and practise democratic/collectivist principles. The main characteristics of a cooperative are as follows:

- the business is owned and controlled by those working in it;
- membership is usually open to all employees, but sometimes subject to special conditions;
- profits are not shared on the basis of the amount of capital put into the business by an individual. Rather, they are distributed in proportion with the amount of work done by each member.

BUSINESS NAMES

If you intend to set up in business as a sole trader using your own name, you will have no problems in this area. However, to project a better image to

You cannot trade under any name you wish. There are certain names that you cannot use.

237

your market and suppliers, you may wish to trade under a business name.

You cannot trade under any name you wish. There are certain names that you cannot use because they may imply you are something that you are not. The Department of Trade and industry produces a useful leaflet called *Business Names – Guidance Notes*, which lists some 90 words, such as 'royal' and 'authority', that you cannot use without official clearance.

If you trade under a business name, then you must display on your premises, letterheads, invoices, sales receipts and so on the following information:

- business name;
- your name (and the name of partners if a partnership or full name of company in the case of a limited company);
- your permanent business address.

When choosing a business name, you should also take care that you do not take unfair advantage of a competitor by selecting a similar one and 'cashing in' on their reputation/goodwill or you could find yourself in court!

PROTECTING YOURSELF AND YOUR BUSINESS

■ Trademarks and patents

There are various methods of protecting your business from unfair competition. If your idea is original in some way and if you think it could be easily copied by a competitor, you may consider investigating the possibility of applying for a patent or registering a trade mark. However, be warned – it can be a difficult and costly business proving that somebody has copied your idea. As a small business, could you afford the legal expenses? One good idea is to check with the Trade Marks Registry that the logo or name you intend to use is not already registered by somebody who can afford legal action.

■ Insurance

You can insure almost anything against any eventuality if you are prepared to pay the price!

From a practical point of view, you should have adequate insurance to cover:

- **public liability** to cover legal liability for death, injury or illness to a member of the public caused by defects in your premises, products, services or by negligence by you or your employees;
- **employer's liability** this is similar to public liability and covers legal claims by your employees – you are forced to take out this cover by law;
- **professional liability** applicable to businesses such as management consultants who may unwittingly or negligently give the wrong advice to a client;
- **personal accident insurance** should be taken out to cover your future financial security in the event of a disabling illness or accident, and you may wish to take out additional cover for employees engaged in potentially dangerous work;
- **goods in transit** applicable to businesses that despatch expensive goods to customers; the goods will be your risk until they reach the customer;
- **Bad debts** the premiums can be expensive, but worth while if a large proportion of your credit sales are with a few customers – think about what would happen to your business if one of them went bankrupt;
- **fire, flood, storm, water damage, consequential loss of profits, commercial use of motor cars** check all your assets, from premises to cash, are properly covered, and remember, if your business is closed down for a month due to, say, fire damage, your overheads will still mount up and profits from sales will be lost – will you be covered for this?

It is wise to shop around for the best deal on price, payment terms and quality of cover.

TAX MATTERS

■ Income tax

There are two things you would be well advised to do before starting in business.

- Employ the services of a good accountant. This does not mean that you should not keep your own books, but, rather, dealing with the Inland Revenue is in many cases best left to the professional. At the very least, you will need advice from your accountant on the best kind of bookkeeping system to use, choice of accounting date (the date when you draw up your final accounts) and the tax rules governing what you can and cannot offset against tax.

> *Employ the services of a good accountant.*

- Inform your local Inland Revenue offices of the date you intend to commence trading. This, if nothing else, gets your relationship with the Inland Revenue off to a good start. It will also supply you with a booklet entitled *Starting in Business,* giving you an overview of taxation and the self-employed.

As previously noted, if you start in business as a sole trader or partnership, you will be taxed on your net profits as shown in your profit and loss account. However, it is possible that the Inland Revenue will slightly adjust the net profit figure because of special rules it applies to the calculation of depreciation on certain assets for tax purposes. Your accountant will advise you of the details and make the necessary adjustments if required. As for the rate of tax you are charged and your tax coding (personal allowances), there is no difference between self-employment and employment.

Besides the nature of the allowances you can claim, the main difference between employment and self-employment for tax purposes is the time period of the earnings/profits on which your tax is based and the payment dates. As you will be aware, as an employed person your tax is calculated on your weekly or monthly earnings. As a self-employed person the rules are different and quite complicated.

It is beyond the scope of this book to deal with the full complexities of taxation. Save to say, it is worth spending some time completing your tax returns and so on.

Value added tax

References have already been made to VAT in earlier chapters, so the following is a brief reminder of what you need to do. First, you should note that an informative and comprehensive pack of free material on this subject is available from your local VAT office (look up the number in your telephone directory).

To the newcomer, VAT can appear to be a horribly complicated tax, but, in essence the principle is quite straightforward; it is the paperwork that goes with it that is laborious and sometimes complicated. It is, in actual fact, a tax on the value you add to goods and services, which is payable by the end purchaser.

Let's take a simple example to demonstrate the process. Take the case of a retailer buying and selling goods on which VAT is payable at 17.5 per cent. Let's imagine the retailer buys goods from a wholesaler at a VAT-exclusive cost of £100. He will actually pay £117.50 (cost price plus 17.5 per cent VAT). Now let's assume he sells all those goods at a mark-up of 100 per cent (profit margin of 50 per cent). He will receive £200 plus 17.5 per cent VAT on the selling prices, a total of £235. The VAT he paid is known as his 'input tax' and is reclaimable; the VAT he charged on the sales, which is known as his 'output tax', is payable to HM Customs and Excise. The VAT actually due is the difference between his output tax of £35 (VAT on sales) and his input tax of £17.50 (VAT on cost of goods), a total of £17.50; which is exactly 17.5 per cent of £100, the value added to the goods.

In theory, the existence of VAT does not affect the profits. If VAT didn't exist, the gross profit would be: £200 (selling price) − £100 (cost price) = £100. With the existence of VAT the same is true and £235 (the amount actually received from sales) − £117.50 (the amount actually paid for stock) = £117.50 (the amount held before payment of VAT) − £17.50 (VAT payable) = £100 gross profit.

It is clear that it is the customer who actually pays the VAT on the value you added to the stock and it is you who has collected the tax on behalf of the Customs and Excise. The existence of VAT, by forcing the consumer to incur extra expenditure, indirectly reduces overall sales and, therefore, profits.

The following are important points to note about VAT:

- you must be registered for VAT if you expect your sales of applicable items to exceed the VAT threshold in any quarter or 12-month period;
- it is your responsibility to register for VAT – it is not considered a valid excuse to say you did not realise your turnover would be 'that large', the Customs and Excise will still demand the VAT due even if you haven't charged it;
- Customs and Excise has wide-ranging powers of search and entry and any attempt to defraud them can easily lead to a prison sentence.
- You will need proof of all your inputs and outputs;
- if you are not sure about any aspect of VAT in relation to your business, contact your local VAT office before you make a complete mess of things – they will be only too pleased to help as it is in their interests for you to get it right at the outset;
- in some instances, it can actually be beneficial for a business to be registered because VAT paid on some capital items can be recovered.

OTHER LEGAL CONSIDERATIONS

■ Licences

Registration, permission or a licence is required under the law for some business activities; for others it may be desirable but not legally necessary. If your business will involve any of the following activities, then you certainly should be recommended to seek legal advice:

- nursing care;
- employing or care of children;
- credit and loan activities;
- gambling;

- employment agencies;
- change of use of premises.

Many other activities – such as door-to-door selling, taxi licences, food and catering – are covered by local and national government legislation and bodies. In all cases you should consult and check with the following to see if any permission, licences or registration are required:

- planning department;
- environmental health;
- Trading Standards Office;
- police;
- Clerk to the Justices (licensed premises).

If you are still unsure, check with your solicitor.

■ Consumer legislation

There are comprehensive laws in existence to protect the rights of the consumer. You should make sure that your trading policy adheres to them. Otherwise, two serious consequences might result:
- prosecution;
- loss of reputation and customer goodwill, particularly if the incident is reported in the local press.

Contact your local Trading Standards Office who will provide you with useful free booklets and further advice if you need it.

The main pieces of legislation that concern most businesses are the Consumer Protection Act, the Sale of Goods and Services Act, the Trade Descriptions Act, the Weights and Measures Act, the Consumer Safety Act, the Consumer Credit Act and the Food Hygiene Regulations. These collectively make it an offence to sell or manufacture goods that are unfit for human consumption, not correctly described, unsafe, of incorrect measure, unfit for the purpose for which they were sold and not of merchantable quality (not to generally accepted standards).

It is very important that you find out and adhere to the legislation that affects your particular business. You will get all the advice you need on this subject from the appropriate department of your local authority – make use of it! Many traders don't and still display illegal signs, such as 'No refunds given', make false statements, sell goods that have passed their 'sell by' date, produce misleading advertisements, and so on. What such illegal actions are doing to their sales is incalculable and in any case, it is just a matter of time before they end up in court!

■ Contracts

Every time you buy or sell something, either in business or in your private life, you enter into a contract that can be written, verbal or both. A contract exists as soon as an offer to sell or buy is made and accepted by both parties. Any statement made about the goods and services pertinent to the transaction during the course of the sale becomes part of the terms of the contract. If either of the parties to the contract feels that the terms have been broken,

> *A contract exists as soon as an offer to sell or buy is made and accepted by both parties.*

then they can attempt to settle the matter by civil action in the courts. It is therefore advisable that your general terms of trade are vetted by a solicitor before you commence business and that they appear on all the necessary purchase and sales documentation that you plan to use.

■ Employment legislation

Employees have comprehensive rights under various Acts of Parliament. However, businesses that only employ a few people or part-timers are exempt from some of the regulations. It is outside the scope of this book to deal with the complicated subject of employment legislation. A range of free booklets on all aspects of employing staff are available from the Advisory Conciliation and Arbitration Service (ACAS), Clifton House, 83-118 Euston Road, London NE1 2RB (tel. 0171-388 5100).

BEFORE YOU START – A CHECKLIST

The following is a broad checklist to help you, as far as possible, to check that you have considered and done all the necessary research and planning before taking the final few steps to starting your business. Some reminders will not be appropriate for the smaller, simpler business whereas for the more complicated operation there is not enough detail here. You may find it a valuable exercise to draw up your own final planning list and certainly a time schedule of the things that have to be done in the last few weeks before you actually open your doors to customers. You will have enough to do then without trying to solve any unforeseen problems and chasing up things you should have done weeks ago.

	Done	Requires more action	When

You and your business

1 Have you selected a business idea that will suit your personality, aptitude, skills and commitments?

2 Have you identified your strengths and weaknesses in relation to running your business?

3 Have you considered and obtained personal insurance to cover accident and sickness?

4 Have you drawn up contingency plans to operate the business if you should become ill or suffer an accident?

The market and sales

1 Have you established what the principal selling points of your business will be?

2 Do you know why customers will buy your products?

	Done	Requires more action	When
3 Have you identified your market segment(s) and detailed their characteristics, including their needs, purchasing power and buying behaviour?			
4 Have you estimated your market share?			
5 Have you produced projected sales figures over your first year's trading?			
6 Do you know the threats and opportunities your competition presents?			
7 Have you decided on how you will distribute (or sell) your product?			
8 Have you fully developed sales promotion to implement at start-up?			
9 Have you developed a trading policy?			
10 Do you know how sensitive your sales will be to fluctuations in price?			
11 Are all your findings about your markets supported by valid and reliable market research?			

Costs

1 Have you anticipated all the costs?			
2 Have you allowed for unforeseen costs?			
3 Do you know when you will incur these costs?			
4 Have you calculated breakeven points for various fluctuations in overheads and variable costs?			

Profit

1 Have you produced profit forecasts?			
2 Have you established your target profits?			

	Done	Requires more action	When

3 Do you know how sensitive your profit is to changes in sales volume, price and costs?

4 Have you built a margin of safety into all your forecasts?

5 Have you projected a rate of return your business will give your capital employed?

Working capital

1 Have you calculated how much working capital your business will require on average?

2 Have you explored ways of reducing the net working capital required?

3 Have you calculated how much working capital will be required to start the business?

4 Have you compiled a cash flow forecast for your first 12 months?

5 Is it based on well-researched facts?

6 Have you taken all possible steps to minimise cash flow problems?

Fixed assets

1 Have you made a detailed checklist to select major fixed assets – say, based on quality, price, reliability, suitability, and so on

2 Have you a detailed list of requirements?

3 Have you researched the alternatives of leasing, renting or buying secondhand?

4 Have you checked availability?

	Done	Requires more action	When

Premises

1 Have you fully researched the location and assessed its suitability for your business?

2 Have you obtained the necessary legal advice?

3 Do you have security of tenure?

4 Do you have the necessary planning permission?

5 Have you taken into account future space requirements?

6 Have you calculated all the costs involved in the purchase or acquisition?

Staff

1 Have you checked out the availability of suitable staff?

2 Have you calculated the full costs of employing staff, including management and administration training recruitment and selection National Insurance contributions employee facilities industrial relations/disputes?

3 Have you considered the criteria you will use to select staff?

4 Have you thought out systems to train and motivate them?

5 Do you understand your main responsibilities to staff as laid out by the Employment and Health and Safety at Work laws?

6 Have you obtained employees' liability insurance cover?

Finance

1 Have you calculated how much you will need, when and for what?

	Done	Requires more action	When

2 Have you attempted to match the right finance to the right use?

3 Have you completed your business plan/loan proposals?

4 Have you had initial discussions with your bank?

5 Do you know from your cash flow the size of overdraft facility you will need?

6 Have you discussed this with your bank?

7 Have you checked the availability of grants?

Tax and legal

1 Have you decided on the legal form of your business?

2 If a partnership, have you had a partnership agreement drawn up and signed?

3 Have you sought legal advice – have you selected a solicitor?

4 Are you aware of the legal controls and restrictions on your business?

5 Does your trading policy or manufacturing process take these legal controls into consideration?

6 Have you checked whether or not you should obtain a licence, planning permission or register your business in some way?

7 Have you checked whether or not you should be registered for VAT?

8 Have you informed the Inland Revenue when you intend to commence trading?

	Done	Requires more action	When
9 Have you made arrangements for payment of class 2 National Insurance contributions?			
10 Have you made plans to cover insurable eventualities?			

Business control and administration

1 Have you chosen a bookkeeping system?

2 Do you know how to use it?

3 Have you selected an accountant?

4 Have you taken action to guard against theft?

5 Have you a stock control system?

6 Have you opened a business bank account?

7 Do you have a system to control cash?

8 Do you have a system to monitor and control debtors?

9 Do you have a system to monitor sales, identify fast and slow sellers?

10 Have you identified suppliers of stock, including their terms and delivery capabilities?

11 Do you have a system to monitor profits?

12 Have you drawn up plans to organise the workload for yourself and your staff?

13 Have you had the necessary business documentation printed?

14 Have you considered in advance how you will tackle routine problems?

15 Have you put together a time schedule, complete with all the major things you will need to do over the weeks before commencement of trading?

Finally, good luck!

Index